HarperCollins*Publishers*
77–85 Fulham Palace Road
London W6 8JB

04 06 08 07 05

11 13 15 14 12

ISBN 0 00 220056 2
Originally published in German as a GU Nature Guide by
Gräfe und Unzer GmbH, Munich

© Gräfe und Unzer GmbH, Munich, 1996
© in this English translation HarperCollins*Publishers*, 1996

Written by Detlef Singer
This edition translated and adapted by Ian Dawson

Cover photograph: Blue Tit, *Parus caeruleus*
From William S. Patton at Bruce Coleman

Printed in Singapore

Collins Nature Guide

GARDEN BIRDS

OF BRITAIN & EUROPE

Detlef Singer

Translated and adapted by
IAN DAWSON

HarperCollinsPublishers

Discover nature

Compared to other animals living around us, which either remain hidden or are active mostly after dark, birds are quite easy to watch, as most of them are active by day, show themselves quite often and can be identified at some distance with the aid of binoculars. Add to this the fact that they often draw attention to themselves by calling or singing: many bird songs are so individual that they immediately give away the owner's identity. These characteristics, together with the often very pleasing appearance and fascinating behaviour of birds, mean that bird study has become popular. Bird lovers are no longer laughed at as 'oddballs', as watching wild birds has become a popular pastime in many countries, especially Britain, Holland and Scandinavia. In contrast to many expensive hobbies, you do not have to dig deep into your pocket to start watching birds: a pair of binoculars, preferably 8 x or 10 x magnification, a good identification guide and a notebook to record details of your sightings are all that is needed to begin.

This new handy pocket-sized Collins Nature Guide *Garden Birds* is the ideal companion for all those who until now have seldom bothered with their local bird life and now want to get to know and identify the most common species. But also the more knowledgeable bird lover who is interested in the lives of our feathered neighbours, will find valuable stimulation for his or her studies. The guide presents more than 100 of the most widespread birds in Europe in 275 superb colour photos; these include not just birds in adult male and female plumages, but also seasonally different plumages and young. A further photo on the left-hand text page shows the nest and eggs of most of the species included.

The detailed, but straightforward text arranged under key headings, details appearance, occurrence and voice as well as breeding and feeding behaviour and gives helpful tips for observation.

The section starting with 'Helping birds in the garden' (p. 152), gives hints about what in particular to look out for when identifying birds, and informs the bird lover about suitable ways to help birds in the garden. At the end of the book the reader will find an illustration which shows a natural bird-friendly garden with various aids to nesting. The list of further reading (p. 158) suggests a small selection of books and sound recordings which offer additional information on bird identification and protection of our garden birds. In the index (p. 156) all species are included under both their English and scientific names.

The author

Detlef Singer has a biology degree, specialising in zoology. As an author, translator and editor of nature writing, he specialises in birds and mammals. He is co-author of Collins Nature Guide *Birds of Britain & Europe*.

The adaptor

Ian Dawson has a degree in languages, and is lucky in being able to combine his passion for birds and books in his job as Librarian with the Royal Society for the Protection of Birds.

Colour-coded identification

6–99   Under the green tab are found the song-
        birds such as larks, swallows, Wren,
        redstarts, thrushes, warblers, flycatchers,
        tits, shrikes, crows, finches, buntings.

100–129 Under the red tab are found the Swift,
         Kingfisher, Hoopoe, Wryneck, woodpeckers,
         Cuckoo, owls, falcons, Sparrowhawk, Pheasant,
         doves and pigeons.

130–151 Under the blue tab are found those
         birds which live on or by water such
         as grebes, Grey Heron, White Stork,
         swans, geese, ducks, geese, rails, gulls.

Glossary

Resident: species of birds which can be seen year round in their breeding
area; some of these species e.g. Nuthatch, remain the whole year on their
territory, others e.g. Coal Tit wander in the winter.

Summer visitors: species of birds which can only be met with in spring and
summer; in the rest of the year they are either on migration or in their
winter quarters.

Partial migrants: species of birds which either leave in autumn for winter
quarters or remain in their breeding areas; thus they can be met with all
year, though numbers in winter may be lower or higher.

Winter visitors: species which do not breed with us, but only spend the
winter here.

Passage migrants: these species appear only at migration times, when
passing through.

Skylark
Alauda arvensis

(Larks)

The Skylark is one of the commonest birds of open countryside. Partial migrant. Birds leave the colder parts of the Continent in winter.

Identification: Larger than House Sparrow (18 cm). Inconspicuously coloured ground-dwelling bird with short rounded crest; trailing edge of wing and outer tail feathers white. Feathers of young look 'scaly'. Does not perch in trees, though often on posts.

Distribution: Almost the whole of Europe with the exception of Iceland and parts of the far north. Winters in western Europe and the Mediterranean.

Voice: Call 'tirr', 'priiut' or 'tschrl'. Song consists of long, sustained trilling and warbling phrases. Prolonged song-flight, often hanging high in the sky for many minutes at a time.

Habitat: Open country, including both cultivated fields and meadows.

Breeding: Double-brooded (April to July). Nest of dry stalks, lined with finer material, hidden in a depression on the ground. 3–4 eggs, heavily-speckled brown, incubated by the female; incubation 11–14 days, young leave nest at 9–10 days, before they are able to fly.

Food: Insects, spiders, small snails, seeds, green plant material.

Miscellany: Skylarks visit regular feeding places at the edges of villages in wintery weather early in the year. In autumn they gather in small or large flocks on harvested fields. The not dissimilar Meadow Pipit is a common winter visitor to inland grassland, including parks and rural gardens.

Woodlark
Lullula arborea

(Larks)

A small lark which often perches on trees. Partial migrant. Present at breeding sites February to October.

Identification: Size of House Sparrow (15 cm), short tail and weak bill. Broad whitish stripe over eyes, black-and-white mark on front edge of wing.

Distribution: The whole of Europe north to southern England and S Sweden. Commonest in W and S Europe; very uncommon in England. Winters in S and W Europe and N Africa.

Voice: Call a ringing 'dadidloi' or 'didlui'. Beautiful sustained territorial song consisting of many soft, melancholic ringing phrases in falling cadences ('Heath Nightingale'). Sings from top of tree or in high, circling flight.

Habitat: Favours dry areas, with a mild climate. Breeds in sandy heathland and open, dry conifer woodland. In southern Europe often in vineyards, orchards and olive groves.

Breeding: Double-brooded (end of March to July). Well hidden, neatly woven nest on ground, built of stalks, moss and hair. 3–5 whitish eggs with fine dense brown speckling, incubated by female; incubation 12–15 days, young fledge at 11–13 days.

Food: Insects, spiders, seeds, green plant material.

Miscellany: Sings often by night. The tips of young conifers broken by the weight of the birds may betray the presence of Woodlarks.

1. Skylark; 2. Skylark clutch; 3. Young Woodlarks in nest; 4. Woodlark

1

2/3

4

Crested Lark

Galerida cristata

(Larks)

The Crested Lark can be recognised by its conspicuous long pointed crest. Resident. Does not occur in Britain.

Identification: A little bigger than House Sparrow (17 cm). Rather long powerful bill; upperparts greyer and less distinctly marked than on Skylark, wings broader and more rounded. Young with shorter crest.

Distribution: Europe except British Isles and Fennoscandia. Commonest in warmer regions.

Voice: Call a soft melodic *'diedidrië'* or *'diu diu diur dli'*. Territorial song of long varied piping and warbling phrases, not so sustained as in the Skylark.

Habitat: Steppes, semi-deserts, and fallow land; often on the edge of built-up areas, sports fields, industrial estates and roadsides.

Breeding: Double-brooded (April to June). Nest of dead plant material, lined with softer material, on ground; often right by busy roads or railways, or even on flat roofs. 3–5 eggs, brooded by the female; incubation 12–14 days, young leave nest at 9–10 days, fledge at 15–16 days.

Food: Chiefly seeds, grain, insects and spiders.

Miscellany: Mostly rather tame. Unlike Skylark and Woodlark, often sings from ground; the song flight swings backwards and forwards.

House Martin

Delichon urbica

(Swallows and martins)

The House Martin is very sociable and our second commonest hirundine. Summer visitor; April to October.

Identification: Distinctly smaller and slimmer than House Sparrow (13 cm). Pure white underparts and rump distinctive. Upperparts glossy blue-black, tail forked. Young with upperparts brown-black and 'dirty' sides to breast.

Distribution: Europe except Iceland. Winters in Africa south of the Sahara.

Voice: Call a frequent *'trr trr'*, *'brriut'* or *'dschrb'*; alarm call a high, piercing *'tsier'*. Song: a medley of chattering and twittering.

Habitat: Nests on buildings, especially in villages and at the edge of towns. Hawks insects over open country and water.

Breeding: Usually double-brooded (May to September). Builds a quarter-ball-shaped nest of mud, with round entrance hole, almost always on the outside of buildings. 4–5 white eggs, sometimes with fine reddish speckling, incubated by both sexes; incubation 14–16 days, young fledge at 22–32 days.

Food: Small flying insects.

Miscellany: Often uses artificial nests. Flight rather erratic and less elegant than Swallow.

1. Crested Lark; 2. Crested Lark nest and eggs; 3. House Martin at nest; 4. House Martin gathering nest material

1

2/3

4

Swallow

Hirundo rustica

(Swallows and martins)

The Swallow is our commonest hirundine. Summer visitor; April to October.

Identification: About House Sparrow size, but distinctly slimmer (19 cm). Very agile and graceful in flight on its long pointed wings. Forehead, chin and throat chestnut, entire upperparts glossy blue-black, except for pale spots on tail. Underparts white with dark breast. Young with short tail-feathers, altogether paler and with grey-brown breast-band.

Distribution: Almost the whole of Europe with the exception of high mountains and the far north. Long-distance migrant, wintering in tropical Africa.

Voice: Call 'vitt vitt' or 'dsched-dsched', alarm call a sharp 'tsivitt tsivitt'. The song consists of continuous twittering, with a mixture of chattering, scratching and musical notes, sounding hurried, and with a purring motif at the end; sings both from a perch and in flight.

Habitat: Nests commonly in villages, farm buildings, and on the edge of towns. Seeks food over meadows and fields, parks and large gardens; in bad weather often over water.

Breeding: Usually double-brooded (May to September). Nest of mud and straw, open above, often with long stalks hanging from the hardened mud structure. Swallows always nest inside buildings, often in cow-sheds or barns. The 4–6 elongated eggs with red speckles are brooded largely by the female; incubation 13–18 days, young fledge at 18–23 days.

Food: Small insects, caught exclusively in flight.

Miscellany: Adults may be recognised by their elongated tail streamers. Like the House Martin, the Swallow gathers small pellets of mud from puddles to build its nest. Drinks in flight from the water surface. Sociable birds which often gather in autumn in large flocks to roost in reedbeds. Sand Martins may nest in pipes in riverbanks in towns, and feed over any suitable waterbodies, including park lakes.

1. Swallows always build their nest inside buildings; 2. Shortly before they fledge, the young stretch right out of the nest as soon as the adult appears with food; (Small picture on left) The eggs are covered with reddish speckles and are rather elongated

1

2

Pied Wagtail

Motacilla alba

(Wagtails)

The Pied Wagtail is our commonest wagtail. Partial migrant in central Europe. Resident in Britain.

Identification: House Sparrow size, but with much longer tail (18 cm). Black, white and grey; females and young paler, as are the males in winter.

Distribution: Almost the whole of Europe, including mountain areas. Winters most numerously in western Europe and Mediterranean region.

Voice: Call a frequent 'tsivlitt', 'psivit' or 'tsitt'. Song an inconspicuous hurried twittering and chattering.

Habitat: A variety of open habitats, mostly near water; also in villages and towns, gardens and playing fields.

Breeding: Mainly double-brooded (April to August). Untidy nest of leaves, stems and moss, often in recess or open hole in buildings, on weirs, in sheds or in wood piles. 5–6 pale grey eggs, thickly speckled darker, brooded mainly by female; incubation 12–14 days, young fledge at 14–15 days.

Food: Mainly insects and spiders taken on the ground, also flying insects.

Miscellany: The Pied Wagtail constantly wags its long tail. Typically runs with jerky head movements. Birds often attack their reflection in windows or car mirrors. Continental birds with pale grey back known as White Wagtail.

Yellow Wagtail

Motacilla flava

(Wagtails)

The Yellow Wagtail is noticeably shorter-tailed than our other wagtails. Summer visitor; April to September.

Identification: House Sparrow size but slimmer and longer tailed (16.5 cm). Throat and head bright yellow (head blue-grey in Continental race), underparts sulphur yellow.

Distribution: Almost all of Europe. Winters in Africa south of the Sahara.

Voice: Call 'psiehp' or 'psewip'. Song unremarkable.

Habitat: Short grass meadows and fields, marshes; often near villages and playing fields.

Breeding: 1–2 broods a year (May to July). Nest on ground, constructed of stems and roots. 5–6 pale-coloured eggs, thickly speckled rusty-yellow; brooded mainly by female; incubation about 13 days, young fledge at 11–13 days.

Food: Grubs and spiders on the ground; catches insects disturbed by grazing animals.

Miscellany: Wags tail almost constantly. Often sits on fence posts or small bushes.

1. Pied (White) Wagtail; 2. Pied (White) Wagtail feeding young; 3. Yellow (Blue-headed) Wagtail; (Small picture on left) Pied Wagtail nest and eggs

Grey Wagtail

Motacilla cinerea

(Wagtails)

The Grey Wagtail is constantly 'wagging' its extra-long tail. Partial migrant; can be met with throughout the year in Britain and Central Europe.

Identification: House Sparrow size, but with very long tail (18 cm); head and upperparts grey, males in breeding plumage with chin and throat black, underparts bright yellow. In female and winter plumage chin and throat whitish.

Distribution: Europe except the north and east. Winters mainly in western and southern Europe.

Voice: Call a loud sharp *'tsiss-tsiss'* or *'tsickick'*. Song of various phrases incorporating call.

Habitat: Streams and rivers, especially in upland regions; also along streams in villages and parks.

Breeding: Double-brooded (April to July). Nest of twigs, grass and moss, close to water, often in recess on bridge or weir.

Food: Insects and their larvae, spiders and worms.

Miscellany: Unlike Pied and Yellow Wagtails, seldom in flocks.

Waxwing

Bombycilla garrulus

(Waxwings)

Waxwings are irruptive winter visitors to Britain and Continental Europe from the far north.

Identification: Smaller than Blackbird (18 cm). Characteristic shining silky plumage and striking crest and wing pattern, black and yellow with sealing-wax-red tips to coverts.

Distribution: Breeds in N Scandinavia and Russia. Wanders erratically in winter to central and southern Europe when food crop fails in the breeding areas.

Voice: Call high trilling *'sirrr'*.

Habitat: Breeds in the spruce and birch forests of the northern taiga. In winter in gardens and parks.

Breeding: Single-brooded (June to July). Nest of twigs and lichen, usually in lichen-draped spruce. 4–6 whitish eggs with dark spots; incubation 14–15 days, young fledge at 14–16 days.

Food: Chiefly berries (especially rowan); when nesting, insects.

Miscellany: The flight silhouette recalls Starling. Waxwings visit berry-bearing shrubs in winter in parks and cemeteries; they are irregular visitors, not appearing every year, though may occur in large flocks.

1. Male Grey Wagtail; 2. Female Grey Wagtail feeding young in nest; 3. Waxwing; (Small picture on left) Grey Wagtail nest and eggs

1

2

3

1 Wren

Troglodytes troglodytes

(Wrens)

The Wren scurries through low bushes like a red-brown mouse. Resident.

Identification: One of our smallest European birds (9.5 cm); tiny and round; plumage brown, finely banded; short tail, often cocked.

Distribution: The whole of Europe except the far north.

Voice: Call a frequent hard *'teck teck teck'* or churring *'tserrrr'*. Song comprises loud warbling and trilling phrases.

Habitat: Undergrowth in woods, thickets and tangles, especially in bushy gardens and parks.

Breeding: Double-brooded (April to July). The male builds several dome-shaped moss nests for the female to choose one from. 5–7 whitish eggs, delicately speckled reddish, and incubated by the female; incubation 14–16 days, young fledge at 15–18 days.

Food: Small insects and their larvae; spiders, worms.

Miscellany: Searches for food mostly near the ground. Often in vicinity of water.

2 Dipper

Cinclus cinclus

(Dippers)

The Dipper is the only songbird that can swim and dive. Resident.

Identification: Plump and short-tailed, smaller than Blackbird (18 cm). Dark brown with striking white bib. Young much paler, lacking clear bib.

Distribution: Patchy distribution in Europe, missing from large parts of the East; mainly in upland regions.

Voice: Call a hard *'tsitt'* or hoarse *'schrett-schrett'*. Song (both sexes) of chattering and harsh scratching noises, often drowned by the sound of rushing water. Also sings in winter.

Habitat: Clear, fast-flowing streams and rivers, including in villages and towns.

Breeding: Double-brooded (March to July). Large dome-shaped nest of moss on rock or wall ledge, between tree roots, or in specially provided nestbox. 4–5 white eggs, brooded by the female; incubation 14–17 days, young fledge at 20–24 days.

Food: Aquatic insects and their larvae, especially caddis-flies.

Miscellany: Bobs regularly on rock in stream. Dives from rock or from surface of water, and swims to bottom to turn over stones in its search for food.

1. Wren; 2. Dipper; 3. Young Dippers; (Small picture on left) Wren at nest

Robin

Erithacus rubecula

(Thrushes)

The Robin is one of the commonest small birds of parks and gardens.
Partial migrant on Continent; British birds resident.

Identification: Smaller than House Sparrow (14 cm), with distinctly longer
legs; large black eyes. Upperparts uniform olive-brown, forehead, throat
and breast brick-red. Young strongly spotted, lacking red.

Distribution: The whole of Europe with the exception of the far north.
Winters mainly in western Europe and around Mediterranean, though
many remain in central Europe.

Voice: Call a hard 'tsick', when alarmed a rapid repeated 'tsiktsiktsik...';
alarm call warning of aerial predator a drawn-out 'tsieh'. Song very rich, a
series of long melancholy phrases, including clear falling rippling notes and
trills. Often sings late into the evening after sunset.

Habitat: Woods with rich undergrowth, copses, scrub, parks and gardens
with trees or bushes; also in villages and towns. Like the Wren, especially
frequent in damp areas.

Breeding: Double-brooded (April to July). Cup-shaped nest of stalks, leaves
and moss, mostly near the ground, concealed between tree roots or low in a
tree hollow or hole in wall. 4–6 pale eggs, with variable, usually rusty,
darker markings, brooded by female. Incubation 14 days, young fledge at
13–14 days.

Food: Insects and their larvae, spiders, worms; in autumn a variety of
berries.

Miscellany: Rather tame; often appears when garden is being dug, attracted
by the insects and worms which are unearthed. When not singing or
searching for food, often concealed in bushes or trees and hard to see. They
are markedly solitary and unsociable. In winter regularly come to bird
tables.

1. In winter Robins are common in parks and gardens where food is put out
for the birds; 2. The young open their beaks wide and show their yellow
throats; 3. Juveniles are heavily spotted and speckled; (Small picture on
left) Nest with eggs

Nightingale

Luscinia megarhynchos

(Thrushes)

The Nightingale is most easily recognised by its loud, richly varied song. Summer visitor; end of April to September.

Identification: A little bigger than House Sparrow (16.5 cm). Plain brown plumage, paler below, without markings; tail reddish-brown. Young strongly spotted.

Distribution: Europe except the north and east. Winters in tropical Africa.

Voice: Alarm call a rising *'hewid'* or a hoarse *'karr'*. Song loud and ringing with rich warbling phrases, and with a characteristic series of rising *'hiu hiu hiu hiu...'* notes followed by *'jugging'*.

Habitat: Deciduous woodland with thick scrub, river banks; also in wild gardens, parks and cemeteries.

Breeding: Single-brooded (May to June). Well hidden nest of dead leaves, stalks and hair, on or near the ground, often in nettles. 4–6 eggs, delicately marked reddish-brown, brooded by female; incubation 13–14 days, young fledge at 11–12 days.

Food: Insects, spiders, snails, worms, berries.

Miscellany: Sings regularly through the night when most other songbirds are silent.

Thrush Nightingale

Luscinia luscinia

(Thrushes)

The Thrush Nightingale replaces Nightingale to the east. Summer visitor; May to September. In Britain rare vagrant.

Identification: Very like Nightingale in size (16.5 cm) and appearance, but upperparts grey-brown, rather than reddish-brown, tail only slightly rufous. Young strongly spotted.

Distribution: Southern Scandinavia, Finland, eastern Europe. Winters in tropical East Africa.

Voice: Call like Nightingale, but deeper *'karr'* and high *'hid'*. Song with slower tempo, deeper pitched, lacking *'jugging'* of Nightingale.

Habitat: Dense vegetation close to water, also in overgrown gardens and parks.

Breeding: Single-brooded (May to June). Nests on ground, nest of old leaves, stalks and twigs, often in a hollow under thick scrub. 4–6 brownish eggs; incubation 13–14 days, young fledge at 10–11 days.

Food: Insects, spiders, snails, worms, berries.

Miscellany: Very hard to see, remaining hidden, its presence betrayed only by its song or call.

1. Nightingale; 2. Nest and eggs of Nightingale; 3. Thrush Nightingale

Dunnock

Prunella modularis

(Accentors)

The Dunnock often remains hidden in thick cover. Partial migrant on Continent. Resident in Britain.

Identification: A little smaller than House Sparrow (14.5 cm), but with thin bill. Inconspicuous in its brown plumage, head and breast blue-grey.

Distribution: Almost the whole of Europe.

Voice: Call a high rather hoarse '*tsieh*' or '*didi*'. Song a continuous thin warbling. Often sings from the tops of young trees, starting early in year, from February or March.

Habitat: Mixed and conifer woods with undergrowth; common in shrubby parkland and gardens.

Breeding: Double-brooded (April to July). Neatly constructed nest of moss in dense cover or young conifers. 4–5 turquoise eggs, brooded by female; incubation 13 days, young fledge at 11–14 days.

Food: Insects, spiders, seeds and berries.

Miscellany: Shuffles along ground in hunched posture. In winter comes to feeding stations.

Black Redstart

Phoenicurus ochruros

(Thrushes)

The Black Redstart is originally a cliff-dweller which now breeds even in the middle of cities. Partial migrant. In Britain scarce.

Identification: A little smaller than House Sparrow (14 cm). Always with rusty-red tail. Male sooty black, with pale patch in wings. Female dark grey-brown. Young brownish, lightly spotted.

Distribution: Europe, with the exception of Iceland, most of British Isles and Scandinavia and N Russia. Winters most commonly around the Mediterranean.

Voice: Alarm call a hard '*hid-teck-teck*', when near nest a repeated '*teckteckteck...*'. Song begins and ends with several whistling notes, around a curious squeezed scratching.

Habitat: Breeds on buildings around farms, in villages and towns.

Breeding: Double-brooded (April to July). Nest of stalks, moss, feathers and hair, often under roofs, in open holes in walls and in artificial nest-holes. 4–6 white eggs, incubated by female; incubation 13–14 days, young fledge at 13–16 days.

Food: Mainly insects.

Miscellany: Bobs frequently and quivers its tail almost constantly. Often sings before dawn from roofs, TV aerials, chimneys and other high song-posts.

1. Dunnock; 2. Female Black Redstart; 3. Recently fledged young Black Redstart; 4. Male Black Redstart; (Small picture on left) Dunnock nest and eggs

1

2/3

4

Redstart

Phoenicurus phoenicurus

(Thrushes)

The Redstart, one of our most beautifully coloured birds, has unfortunately declined in many areas due to habitat change and losses on migration. Summer visitor; end of April to October.

Identification: Long-legged and with rusty tail, like Black Redstart (14 cm). Male strikingly coloured, with forehead gleaming white, throat and sides of head black, underparts rusty-red; in autumn the bright colours are largely hidden by pale feather edges. Female paler than Black Redstart, mainly grey-brown, but still with rusty tail.

Distribution: Europe with the exception of Iceland, Ireland, Greece and parts of the Iberian peninsula. Winters in the savannas of Africa south of the Sahara.

Voice: Call when agitated 'huit' (like Willow Warbler) or 'huid-teck-teck'. Song is a short series of melancholy notes starting with a drawn-out whistle. Also imitates other birds. Sings persistently from before dawn from the top of a tree or prominent song-post.

Habitat: Open deciduous and mixed woodland, gardens with mature trees, parks, cemeteries and orchards; also sometimes in villages.

Breeding: 1–2 broods (May to July). Loose nest of stalks, roots and moss in hole in tree or wall or in tit nestbox. 5–7 green-blue eggs, brooded mainly by female. Incubation 13–14 days, young fledge at 12–15 days.

Food: Insects and their larvae: occasionally berries.

Miscellany: Often flies out after insects from a low branch and returns to the same perch. In the right habitat it may be attracted by providing suitable nestboxes. The entrance hole should if possible be an elongated oval, perhaps because of the bird's long legs.

1. The male Redstart is one of our most colourful birds; 2. In autumn the bright colours of the head and breast are obscured by pale feather edges; 3. In her plain dress the female is inconspicuous; (Small picture on left) Favourite nesting sites are tree cavities with an oval entrance hole

1

2

3

Blackbird   *Turdus merula*

(Thrushes)

The Blackbird is one of the commonest songbirds in parks and gardens; originally purely a woodland bird, this species has adapted very well to live in close association with man. Partial migrant on the Continent; resident numbers in Britain swollen in winter by immigrants.

Identification: (25 cm). Male uniformly black with orange-yellow bill and eye-ring. Female dark brown with rather paler throat and breast. Individuals with patches of white feathers (partial albinos) are not uncommon. Young reddish-brown with strong spotting on underparts. Hops along the ground, unlike Starling.

Distribution: The whole of Europe with the exception of northern Scandinavia and north Russia, though only in winter in Iceland. Many Blackbirds move to western and southern Europe to winter.

Voice: Alarm call 'tak tak' or 'tixtix', which is accelerated into a shrill scolding when very agitated. When threatened from air a high drawn out 'tsieh', or by ground predator a muted 'duk duk'. Song very melodic and varied with flute-like and twittering notes; most phrases have a rather squeezed conclusion.

Habitat: All types of woodland and copses with undergrowth; very common in gardens, parks and cemeteries, even in tiny parks in the middle of cities.

Breeding: 2–3 broods (March to August). Large solid nest of stems and roots, reinforced with damp earth and then lined with further stems; often pieces of plastic and other human detritus are incorporated in the nest. Nest in trees or bushes, in hedges, against overgrown house walls or on balconies. 3–5 blue-green eggs, finely speckled brownish, and brooded mainly by female. Incubation 12–14 days, young fledge at 13–15 days.

Food: Chiefly earthworms; snails, insects, spiders, berries and other fruits.

Miscellany: Blackbirds sing at dawn from tree tops, house roofs or TV aerials – mostly from February, though sometimes as early as December in towns and cities where there is bright lighting.

1. The male Blackbird is easily recognised by his black plumage, yellow bill and eye-ring; 2. The dark brown female gathers large quantities of stalks to build the nest; 3. Young Blackbirds are strongly speckled; (Small picture on left) Two young have already hatched in this nest

1

2

3

Fieldfare

Turdus pilaris

(Thrushes)

Our most colourful thrush. Partial migrant on Continent. In Britain a visitor from October to April.

Identification: Rather bigger than Blackbird (25.5 cm). Recognised on the ground by grey head, chestnut-brown back and black tail; in flight easy to identify with the contrast between black tail, grey rump and white underwing coverts.

Distribution: Northern, central and eastern Europe; many Fieldfares from northern part of range winter in central, southern and western Europe.

Voice: Flight call a repeated '*schack-schack-schack*', when danger threatens a scratching '*trrtrrtrr*'. Song a squeezed scratchy warbling, often in flight.

Habitat: Open deciduous and mixed woodland; often in parks and gardens with mature trees.

Breeding: Sometimes double-brooded (April to June). Nests in trees in loose colonies. 4–6 greenish-blue eggs with reddish pattern. Only the female incubates; incubation 11–14 days, young fledge at 13–14 days.

Food: Worms, snails, insects, berries and fruit.

Miscellany: The Fieldfare is very gregarious and is often met with in flocks. Like the Blackbird usually feeds on the ground, though in winter also regularly in bushes and trees.

Redwing

Turdus iliacus

(Thrushes)

The Redwing breeds in northern Europe and appears with us in winter (October to April).

Identification: Distinctly smaller than Blackbird (21 cm). Flanks red-chestnut, striking cream-coloured stripe over eye; breast striped, not spotted. In flight the chestnut underwing coverts are conspicuous.

Distribution: Iceland, north and northeast Europe. Winters in central, western and southern Europe as far as North Africa.

Voice: Call a high, drawn out, rather hoarse '*tsiieh*'. Song a series of falling whistling notes, followed by a squeezed scratching warble.

Habitat: Breeds chiefly in the northern taiga forest; in winter in fields and hedges, including parks and gardens with berry bushes.

Breeding: 1–2 broods (May to July). Solid tree nest, also on ground in tundra. 5–6 eggs, finely marked with reddish-brown.

Food: Worms, snails, berries, including grapes.

Miscellany: Often in mixed flocks with Fieldfares. Characteristic flight call of migrating birds can often be heard overhead on late October nights.

1. Fieldfare in winter; 2. Fieldfare nest with almost fledged young;
3. Redwing

1

2

3

Song Thrush *Turdus philomelos*

(Thrushes)

One of the commonest songbirds in park and garden, though numbers declining. Resident. Summer visitor to northern and eastern Europe.

Identification: Smaller than Blackbird (23 cm). Easily recognised on the ground by its brown upperparts and cream-coloured, heavily spotted underparts, in flight by its orange-yellow underwing coverts.

Distribution: Europe except Iceland and the greater part of the Iberian peninsula. Winters in southern and western Europe and North Africa.

Voice: Flight call a short sharp '*tsip*'; when danger threatens a penetrating scolding '*dickdickdick...*'. Song consists of varied musical phrases which are repeated from two to four times.

Habitat: Woods and copses with good shrub layer; common in parks and gardens.

Breeding: Double-brooded (April to July). Strong, bowl-shaped nest, lined with mud and rotten wood, often in a young tree. 3–6 striking pale blue eggs, brooded by the female; incubation 12–14 days, young fledge at 14–16 days.

Food: Worms, snails, insects, berries, fruit.

Miscellany: Sings mainly in the early morning and evenings. Breaks open garden snails on a stone, the so-called 'thrushes' anvil'.

Mistle Thrush *Turdus viscivorus*

(Thrushes)

The Mistle Thrush is our largest thrush. Partial migrant on Continent. Resident in Britain.

Identification: Similar to Song Thrush, but much bigger (27 cm). Upperparts more grey-brown, coarser spotting below.

Distribution: Almost the whole of Europe except for Iceland and parts of Scandinavia. Winters mainly in western and southern Europe.

Voice: Flight call a hard grating '*trrrr*'. Song recalls Blackbird, but less varied, with longer pauses between phrases, and with melancholy tone.

Habitat: Open woodland, and parkland and gardens with trees.

Breeding: Double-brooded (March to July). Large nest strengthened with earth, built in a tree. 3–5 bluish eggs with reddish flecks, brooded by female. Incubation 12–15 days, young fledge at 12–15 days.

Food: Worms, snails, insects, berries.

Miscellany: Sings from February. In winter often defends berried trees and bushes.

1. Song Thrush; 2. Young Song Thrush; 3. Mistle Thrush; (Small picture on left) Song Thrush nest and eggs

1

2

3

Icterine Warbler

Hippolais icterina

(Warblers)

The Icterine Warbler imitates the voices of so many other birds, that it makes up an entire bird choir by itself. Summer visitor; May to August. In Britain only a scarce migrant.

Identification: Smaller than House Sparrow (13 cm). Characteristic are the slender Reed Warbler-like build, the long robust orange-coloured bill, and the striking yellow underparts. Upperparts olive brown.

Distribution: Central and eastern Europe to the Balkans in the southeast and central Scandinavia in the north. Winters in tropical Africa.

Voice: Call a characteristic three-syllable *'dederoid'* or *'dje-dje-dje-liu'*. Alarm call a smacking *'tze tze tze'*. Loud and varied song combines scratchy and sweet notes and includes excellent mimicry of, for example swallows, tits, thrushes, Golden Oriole, Chaffinch, House and Tree Sparrows.

Habitat: Open deciduous woodland and copses; frequent in large gardens with good cover, and parkland.

Breeding: Single-brooded (May to July). Tidy cup-shaped nest constructed of stalks, leaves and bark, firmly lodged in a fork, 2–4 m high. 4–6 pink eggs with black speckles, brooded by both sexes; incubation 13–14 days, young fledge at 13–15 days.

Food: Insects and spiders, in late summer also berries.

Miscellany: The Icterine Warbler is attracted to gardens with dense, tall shrubs. When setting up territory the male sings almost the entire day with wide open bill, moving its head from side to side, and hopping from twig to twig.

1. Male Icterine Warbler; 2. Icterine Warbler at nest with young; (Small picture on left) The pink-coloured eggs in the prettily woven nest are speckled black

Reed Warbler

Acrocephalus scirpaceus

(Warblers)

The Reed Warbler also breeds in narrow strips of reeds by park lakes as well as reedbeds. Summer visitor; May to September.

Identification: Smaller than House Sparrow (13 cm). Upperparts warm toned, with reddish-brown rump, dark legs.

Distribution: Europe north to England, southern Scandinavia and south Finland. Winters in tropical Africa.

Voice: When disturbed a hard *'ved'* or deep *'kresh'*. The rhythmical song consists of melodic and scratchy phrases, each repeated two or three times.

Habitat: Reedbeds and reed fringe of water bodies.

Breeding: 1–2 broods (May to August). Deep nest woven between upright reed stems, usually 1–1.5 m above the water. 3–5 pale greenish eggs with heavy brownish speckling, incubated by female; incubation 11–12 days, young fledge at 10–12 days.

Food: Insects, spiders.

Miscellany: On migration the Reed Warbler can be met with in bushes far from water. The related Sedge Warbler usually nests by water, often in parks.

Garden Warbler

Sylvia borin

(Warblers)

The very inconspicuous Garden Warbler shows no special plumage features. Summer visitor; May to September.

Identification: Smaller than House Sparrow (14 cm). Upperparts uniform olive-brown with paler underparts; rather rounded head, bill and tail relatively short.

Distribution: Europe apart from the Mediterranean coast and the far north. Winters in Africa south of the Sahara.

Voice: Alarm call *'vet vet vet'*. Song loud and melodious in continuous chattering phrases with organ-like notes.

Habitat: Thick scrub, woods and parks with plenty of undergrowth, overgrown gardens.

Breeding: Single-brooded (May to July). Loose nest of stalks and roots, mostly low in thick undergrowth. 4–5 eggs irregularly speckled brownish, incubated by both sexes; incubation 11–13 days, young fledge at 10–12 days.

Food: Insects, spiders, and in autumn many berries.

Miscellany: Unless familiar with the song, the Garden Warbler can be difficult to find as it favours thick scrub and even when singing remains inconspicuous.

1. Reed Warbler; 2. Young Reed Warblers in nest; 3. Garden Warbler feeding young; (Small picture on left) Nest and eggs of Garden Warbler

1 Lesser Whitethroat

Sylvia curruca

(Warblers)

The Lesser Whitethroat is a frequent visitor to lowland Britain arriving from the southeast. Summer visitor; April to October.

Identification: Smaller than House Sparrow (13.5 cm). Upperparts brown-grey, wings browner; grey crown with ear-coverts dark grey, throat white.

Distribution: Europe west to France and England, north to central Scandinavia. Winters in east Africa south of the Sahara.

Voice: Call when agitated a repeated '*tek*' or '*tjeck*'. Song a monotonous rattling phrase following a soft hurried warble.

Habitat: Gardens and parks, cemeteries, woodland edge and orchards.

Breeding: Single-brooded (May to July). Flimsy, shallow nest in conifers or thick scrub. 4–6 eggs speckled in several colours, brooded by both sexes; incubation 11–12 days, young fledge at 10–12 days.

Food: Insects, spiders, berries.

Miscellany: Unlike its relative, the Common Whitethroat, often remains hidden, only drawing attention to itself by its rattling song.

2 Common Whitethroat

Sylvia communis

(Warblers)

The Whitethroat was very abundant in hedges and farmland before 1968, when the population crashed. Numbers have only partly recovered.

Identification: Smaller than House Sparrow (14 cm). The rusty brown wings, narrow white eye-ring and pale legs are characteristic. Male with grey head, that of female brown.

Distribution: Europe except for Iceland, northern Scandinavia and northern Russia. Winters in Africa south of Sahara.

Voice: Call a repeated '*void void...*' or '*tek*'. Song consists of short, harsh chattering and scratchy phrases.

Habitat: Lives in open countryside with thorn scrub and in thorny hedges; also on roadside verges and in overgrown gardens and open parkland.

Breeding: Double-brooded (May to July). Nest of dry stalks and roots, mostly low in thorn scrub. 4–5 pale grey eggs, finely spotted, incubated by both sexes; incubation 11–13 days, young fledge at 11–12 days.

Food: Insects, spiders, in autumn also berries.

Miscellany: The male is often noticed when he flies up from the top of a bush in his short song flight.

1. Singing male Lesser Whitethroat;
2. Singing male Common Whitethroat; (Small picture on left) Nest and eggs of Common Whitethroat

1

2

Blackcap

(Warblers)

Sylvia atricapilla

The Blackcap is one of our commonest warblers. Chiefly summer visitor; April to October. In Britain small numbers also winter.

Identification: Smaller than House Sparrow (14 cm). Rather plain coloured warbler, male grey with clearly demarcated black skullcap, wings rather darker grey-brown, underparts ash-grey; female browner and with rusty-brown cap, young with red-brown cap. In their first autumn, many males are identifiable by red-brown flecks in their otherwise already black cap.

Distribution: Almost the whole of Europe except Iceland and the north of Fennoscandia. Winters in North Africa as well as western and southern Europe north to Britain.

Voice: Call when disturbed a hard 'tek tek tek', which accelerates into a chattering when very agitated. The song is one of our finest bird songs – full musical flute-like notes which abruptly follow a series of hurried warbling notes. The song of the Garden Warbler is very similar.

Habitat: Woodland with well developed cover, shrub-rich parks and gardens, even in town centres. More regularly met with in gardens than the Garden Warbler!

Breeding: Double-brooded (late April to July). Loose, shallow nest of grass, thin roots and some moss, low in a bush or young tree, usually below 1.5 m; the edge of the nest is so well interwoven with the surrounding vegetation that it is very difficult to find (only worth searching in autumn and winter!). 4–6 pale brown eggs, speckled darker, incubated by both sexes; incubation 11–15 days, young fledge at 10–14 days.

Food: Insects and spiders; in autumn various berries.

Miscellany: Lives in cover, and usually heard before seen. When breeding Blackcaps are easily disturbed and often abandon their nest.

1. The male is easily recognised with his black skullcap; 2. The female (right) has a rusty-brown cap. Both parents feed the young; 3. Young male bathing; (Small picture on left) Nest and eggs

1

2

3

Sardinian Warbler

Sylvia melanocephala

(Warblers)

The Sardinian Warbler is a typical inhabitant of the Mediterranean region. Resident; rare vagrant further north, including to Britain.

Identification: Smaller than House Sparrow (13 cm). A robust warbler with short wings and red eye-ring. Males predominantly grey with velvety-black head, females with grey head.

Distribution: Countries bordering the Mediterranean, Portugal to Turkey.

Voice: Alarm call a loud '*trett-trett-trett-trett*'. Song of short ringing phrases strung together with a mixture of grating, noisy and musical notes.

Habitat: Mediterranean scrub, maquis, and woods with thick undergrowth.

Breeding: Double-brooded (March to July). Relatively solid nest low in scrub. 3–5 eggs, delicately speckled darker; incubation 12–14 days, young fledge at 12–13 days.

Food: Insects, spiders, berries and other fruit.

Miscellany: The Sardinian Warbler usually draws attention to its presence with its sudden, loud, harsh alarm rattle.

Wood Warbler

Phylloscopus sibilatrix

(Warblers)

The Wood Warbler is a characteristic bird of mature beech forest and sessile oak woodland. Summer visitor; April to September.

Identification: Smaller than House Sparrow (12.5 cm). Easily recognised by its strongly yellowish-green upperparts, the gleaming yellow of throat and breast and the pure white of the rest of the underparts; also the sulphur yellow supercilium.

Distribution: Europe apart from the Iberian peninsula, Iceland, Ireland, northern Scandinavia and Greece.

Voice: When disturbed a soft '*diuh*'. Song a shivering trill, which begins with a series of accelerating '*sip*' notes; alternative song phrase of plaintive falling notes '*diu-diu-diu-diu...*'.

Habitat: Favours mature beech forest, also in mixed woods, parks and large gardens with mature beeches and sparse ground cover.

Breeding: Single-brooded (May to June). Dome-shaped nest (like bread oven) of leaves and grass on or close to ground, often hidden in dead leaves. 5–7 whitish eggs with red and brown speckling, incubated by female;

incubation 13–14 days, young fledge at 11–13 days.

Food: Insects and spiders.

Miscellany: Sings from horizontal branches in the lower canopy, the bird also holding its body horizontal; often flies to another branch while still singing.

1. Male Sardinian Warbler; 2. Wood Warbler; (Small picture on left) Nest and eggs of Sardinian Warbler

Chiffchaff
Phylloscopus collybita
(Warblers)

The Chiffchaff is one of the commonest small birds of parks and gardens. Summer visitor; March to November. Small numbers also winter in Britain.
Identification: Smaller than House Sparrow (11 cm). More olive-brown, less yellow than Willow Warbler; pale supercilium, legs dark.
Distribution: Europe apart from Iceland, parts of Scandinavia and the Iberian peninsula. Winters in southern Europe and Africa.
Voice: Call a monosyllabic *'heud'*. Very distinctive and easily recognised song: *'tsilp-tsalp-tselp-tsilp...'*.
Habitat: Open deciduous and mixed woodland, with undergrowth; common in larger gardens and parks with trees.
Breeding: 1–2 broods (April to July). Dome-shaped 'bread oven' nest of dry leaves and stalks, built in thick vegetation close to ground. 5–6 eggs speckled yellowish to brownish, incubated by female; incubation 13–15 days, young fledge at 14–16 days.
Food: Insects and spiders.
Miscellany: Often sings from willows and birches.

Willow Warbler
Phylloscopus trochilus
(Warblers)

The Willow Warbler is catholic in its choice of habitat and is common in almost all types of woodland. Summer visitor; April to October.
Identification: Smaller than House Sparrow (11.5 cm). Difficult to distinguish from Chiffchaff, the most important difference after the song being the pale legs. Underparts and supercilium, especially in young birds in autumn, with more yellow.
Distribution: Europe apart from Iceland and the entire south. Winters in Africa south of the Sahara.
Voice: Call similar to Chiffchaff but distinctly disyllabic *'hu-id'*. Song a soft falling phrase of pure notes of melancholy character – somewhat reminiscent of Chaffinch, but much softer.
Habitat: Light deciduous and mixed woodland, osier-beds; common in parks, cemeteries and large gardens with scrub, willows and birches.
Breeding: 1–2 broods (May to July). Dome-shaped 'bread oven' nest of stems and moss, lined with many feathers, hidden among tall grass. 4–7 reddish-speckled eggs, brooded by female; incubation 13–14 days, young fledge at 12–15 days.
Food: Insects and spiders.
Miscellany: Does not flutter about in the foliage quite so restlessly as Chiffchaff.

1. The Chiffchaff has dark legs ...; 2. ... and the Willow Warbler pale legs; (Small picture on left) Young Chiffchaffs

1 Goldcrest
Regulus regulus
(Warblers)

The Goldcrest is not only the smallest European bird, but one of the smallest in the world. Resident.

Identification: (9 cm). The broad yellow, black bordered, central crown stripe, also with some orange feathers in the male, is characteristic; lacks eyestripe and supercilium of next species.

Distribution: Europe apart from Iceland, northern Scandinavia and most of the Iberian peninsula.

Voice: Call a thin 'sih-sih-sih'. Song of short phrases of very high-pitched notes, alternating in pitch, and finishing with a pronounced deeper flourish.

Habitat: Mainly spruce woods; common in parks and cemeteries, also large gardens, with conifers.

Breeding: Double-brooded (April to June). Compact, cup-shaped moss nest in a conifer fork or suspended from a branch. 8–10 eggs, finely marked with brownish, brooded by female; incubation 16 days, young fledge at 19 days.

Food: Tiny insects and spiders.

Miscellany: Often met with in winter in company of roving flocks of tits and treecreepers.

2 Firecrest
Regulus ignicapillus
(Warblers)

The Firecrest is no larger than its close relative. Summer visitor; March to October. In Britain scarce, mainly on passage.

Identification: Tiny (9 cm). Distinguished from the Goldcrest by the black stripe through and white stripe over the eye. Crown in male orange-red.

Distribution: Europe apart from Iceland, Scandinavia, most of Britain and eastern Europe.

Voice: Call a high piercing 'sisisi'. Song a high-pitched rapid 'sisisisisisitt'.

Habitat: Less strongly tied to conifers than Goldcrest, also occurring in parks and gardens with few conifers.

Breeding: Double-brooded (May to July). Elaborate thick-walled cup-nest of moss and spiders webs – mostly on the underside of a conifer branch. 7–12 eggs, incubated by female; incubation 14–16 days, young fledge at 20–24 days.

Food: Insects and spiders.

Miscellany: Both crests are often amazingly confiding and come very close. They occasionally hover at the ends of branches. Compared to its relative, the Firecrest seeks food more often on the upper side of twigs.

1. Male Goldcrest; 2. Male Firecrest; (Small picture on left) Firecrest nest and eggs

Pied Flycatcher *Ficedula hypoleuca*

(Flycatchers)

A common park and garden bird on the Continent, though chiefly a bird of western oakwoods in Britain. Summer visitor; April to September.

Identification: Smaller than House Sparrow (13 cm). In Britain, the Alps and northern Europe, males contrastingly black and white; by contrast males from central European populations greyish-brown and white, like the females, but with white forehead in spring.

Distribution: Europe except Iceland and the greater part of southern Europe. Winters in tropical Africa.

Voice: Call a frequent '*bitt*' or warning '*tzeck*'. Song of clear rather melancholy rising and falling notes.

Habitat: A variety of mature woodland types; also in parks and gardens with mature trees.

Breeding: Single-brooded (May to June). Nests in tree holes and nestboxes. 6–8 pale blue eggs, brooded by female; incubation 13–15 days, young fledge at 14–17 days.

Food: Flying insects.

Miscellany: Pied Flycatchers readily use nestboxes and are relatively easy to attract to breed in woods and parks within their range.

Collared Flycatcher *Ficedula albicollis*

(Flycatchers)

The Collared Flycatcher is one of Europe's most striking small birds. Summer visitor; April to September. A rare vagrant to Britain.

Identification: Smaller than House Sparrow (13 cm). Old breeding males always black-and-white, from male Pied Flycatcher by white neck collar, more white in wing and white rump; females of both species very similar.

Distribution: An eastern species, ranging from central to eastern Europe, also Italy. Winters in Africa south of the Sahara.

Voice: Call an extended high indrawn '*hieb*'. Song slower and more squeezed than that of Pied Flycatcher.

Habitat: Deciduous and mixed woodland, parks and large gardens with mature oak trees.

Breeding: Single-brooded (May to June). Nests in tree holes and nestboxes. 5–7 pale bluish eggs, brooded by female; incubation 12–14 days, young fledge at 15–18 days.

Food: Flying insects.

Miscellany: The Collared Flycatcher regularly breeds in nestboxes. Hunts high in the canopy for insects.

1. Male Pied Flycatcher; 2. Female Pied Flycatcher; 3. Female Collared Flycatcher; 4. Male Collared Flycatcher; (Small picture on left) Collared Flycatcher clutch

Red-breasted Flycatcher
Ficedula parva

(Flycatchers)

The Red-breasted Flycatcher resembles a small Robin. Summer visitor;
May to September. In Britain only a scarce autumn migrant.

Identification: Smaller than Pied and Collared Flycatchers (11.5 cm).
Conspicuous white patches at base of tail. Males do not attain red throat
and breast until third year; before then indistinguishable from females.

Distribution: An eastern species, occurring west as far as southern Sweden
and Germany, where patchily distributed. Winters in India and Pakistan.

Voice: Call a repeated 'tsit'. Song of silvery falling phrases, which at a
distance recalls that of Willow Warbler.

Habitat: Damp, ancient deciduous woodland; similar parkland habitat.

Breeding: Single-brooded (May to June). Nests in open holes and crevices
in tree trunks. 5–6 whitish eggs, with delicate brownish speckling;
incubated by female; incubation 13 days, young fledge at 13–14 days.

Food: Flying insects.

Miscellany: The Red-breasted Flycatcher is difficult to find without
knowing its song, as it hunts for insects mainly in the tree canopy.

Spotted Flycatcher
Muscicapa striata

(Flycatchers)

The Spotted Flycatcher is our commonest flycatcher. Summer visitor; April
to September.

Identification: Smaller than House Sparrow (14 cm). Inconspicuous
grey-brown plumage, underparts paler; forehead and breast finely streaked.
Upperparts of young with pale spots, underparts with darker markings.

Distribution: Europe except Iceland. Winters in southern half of Africa.

Voice: Call a repeated 'pst', 'tsek' or 'tsi-tek-tek'. Song, easily overlooked, of
clipped high chirping notes.

Habitat: Open woods, woodland edge, parks and gardens with mature trees.

Breeding: 1–2 broods (May to August). Loosely constructed nest of moss,
hair and feathers in open hole in tree, wall or in open nestbox. 4–6 pale
greenish eggs, speckled brownish, incubated by female; incubation 12–14
days, young fledge at 12–15 days.

Food: Flying insects.

Miscellany: Sits upright on a lookout perch, from which it flies out to catch
passing insects, before returning
usually to the same perch. Hovers
occasionally.

1. Male Red-breasted Flycatcher; 2.
Adult male Red-breasted Flycatcher
at the nesthole, in which the female
is sitting; 3. Spotted Flycatcher; 4.
Young Spotted Flycatchers; (Small
picture on left) Spotted Flycatcher
clutch

1 Marsh Tit
Parus palustris

(Tits)

The Marsh Tit is not infrequent in parks and gardens with deciduous trees.
Resident.

Identification: Smaller than Great Tit (11.5 cm). Dull grey-brown with (in adults) a shiny black cap.

Distribution: Europe except Iceland, Ireland, the greater part of northern Europe and the Iberian peninsula.

Voice: Call an explosive *'pistyu-dididi'*. Song a series of monotonous repeated notes such as *'diep-diep-diep-diep-diep'* or *'tsietsietsietsietsietsie'*.

Habitat: Deciduous and mixed woods, parks and gardens; despite its name seldom in wet habitats.

Breeding: Single-brooded (April to May). Nest of moss, hair and feathers in tree hole or nestbox. 7–9 reddish-spotted eggs, brooded by female; incubation 13–17 days, young fledge at 17–20 days.

Food: Insects, spiders, weed seeds, thistles.

Miscellany: In autumn Marsh Tits often collect seeds and hide them in crevices in bark as a winter larder.

2 Willow Tit
Parus montanus

(Tits)

Marsh and Willow Tits are almost identical in plumage. Resident.

Identification: Very similar to Marsh Tit (11.5 cm). Distinguished by larger head, matt black (not glossy) cap, and (in winter and spring) pale panel in wing.

Distribution: Europe except Iceland, Ireland, the Iberian and Italian peninsulas.

Voice: Call an extended nasal *'tsi-tsi-deh-deh-deh'*. Song of high-pitched clear whistling notes *'tsiu-tsiu-tsiu...'*.

Habitat: In damper woodland than Marsh Tit and less often in gardens and parks; marshy copses, wooded river banks, upland woods.

Breeding: 1–2 broods (May to June). Nest of moss, hair and small chips of wood, usually in self-excavated hole in tree; also in woodpecker holes and nestboxes. 6–9 white eggs, with fine reddish spots, incubated by female; incubation 13–15 days, young fledge at 17–19 days.

Food: Insects, spiders, small seeds.

Miscellany: The Willow Tit was long overlooked in Britain, being recognised as a different species to Marsh Tit less than 100 years ago.

1. Marsh Tit; 2. Willow Tit

1

2

Blue Tit

Parus caeruleus

(Tits)

The Blue Tit is, along with the Great Tit, our commonest species of tit.
Resident.

Identification: Smaller than Great Tit (11.5 cm). Unmistakable, with its
blue and yellow plumage. Young blue-green and yellowish.

Distribution: Europe except for Iceland and northern Scandinavia.

Voice: Call a repeated '*tsi-tsi-tsi*', when alarmed '*tserrretetetet*'. Song
phrases bright and clear '*tsi-tsi-sirrrr*'.

Habitat: Deciduous and mixed woodland, especially with oaks; common in
gardens and parks.

Breeding: 1–2 broods a year (1 in Britain) (April to June). Felty nest of
moss, wool, hair and feathers in tree hole, nestbox, hole in wall or even in
letter-box. 7–14 white eggs, with reddish spots, brooded by female;
incubation 13–15 days, young fledge at 16–22 days.

Food: Insects, spiders, seeds, nuts, suet.

Miscellany: Hangs skilfully from thin twigs, often belly uppermost. Can
easily be attracted to nest in the garden in nestboxes.

Crested Tit

Parus cristatus

(Tits)

The Crested Tit is strongly associated with conifer woods. Resident. In
Britain almost confined to ancient Caledonian pine forest in northeast
Scotland.

Identification: Smaller than Great Tit (11.5 cm). The pointed crest and
faded grey-brown upperparts are diagnostic.

Distribution: Most of Europe, but absent from Iceland, northern
Scandinavia, most of British Isles and Italy.

Voice: Call a purring '*tsi-tsi-gurrrr*'. Song seldom heard – a series of trilling
and churring notes like the call.

Habitat: Conifer and mixed woodland, also in parks and large gardens with
conifers.

Breeding: 1–2 broods (April to June). Nest of animal and plant wool and
spiders webs, usually in self-excavated, rather narrow tree-hole, also in
woodpecker hole and (rarely) nestboxes. 5–8 reddish-speckled eggs,
incubated by female; incubation 13–16 days, young fledge at 17–21 days.

Food: Insects, spiders, seeds, nuts.

Miscellany: Usually out of sight high
in conifers, first noticed by its
distinctive call. In winter Crested
Tits may visit bird feeders close to
woodland.

1. Blue Tit on suet-ball; 2. Blue Tit
feeding young in nestbox; 3. Female
Blue Tit begging for food to
strengthen pair-bond; 4. Crested
Tit; (Small picture on left) Blue Tit
clutch

Great Tit   *Parus major*

(Tits)

The Great Tit is our largest species of tit and very common in woods, parks and gardens. Resident.

Identification: A little smaller than House Sparrow (14 cm), with robust build. Head black with white cheeks, underparts mainly yellow, male with broad, strong black stripe down centre of breast and belly, female with narrower, less strongly marked stripe. Young with smaller bib and yellowish cheeks, lacking black border below.

Distribution: Europe except Iceland and the far north.

Voice: Call when disturbed a rasping '*tscher-r-r-r*', a Chaffinch-like '*pink*' or '*pink dedede*', '*tsituit*' or '*tsitsitsi*'; often mimics the calls of other tits, such as Marsh Tit. Song usually of two to three syllables, regularly repeated: '*tsi-tsi-beh tsi-tsi-beh...*', or '*tsi-pe tsi-pe...*'. Sings regularly in winter in fine weather.

Habitat: In almost all types of countryside with trees, except pure coniferous woodland. Common in deciduous and mixed woodland; most numerous in gardens, cemeteries and parks, even in the middle of towns; one of our commonest birds.

Breeding: 1–2 broods (April to July). Nests in tree hole, nestbox, hole in wall, occasionally in letter-box or pipes. Nest of moss, stalks, roots and wool, padded with animal and plant wool. 8–12 whitish eggs, covered with reddish speckling, incubated by female; incubation 12–15 days, young fledge at 16–22 days.

Food: The most catholic of all the tits: insects, spiders, nuts, suet, sunflower seeds and other seeds.

Miscellany: Great Tits are quite tame and appear commonly at bird-tables in winter; they often chase other small birds from the feeders. They can be attracted to nest in the garden by making or buying suitable nestboxes with an entrance hole of 32 mm diameter.

1. The Great Tit is one of our commonest garden birds; 2. Young Great Tits in nestbox; 3. Young can be recognised by their yellowish cheeks; (Small picture on left) Nest and eggs

1

2

3

Coal Tit

Parus ater

(Tits)

The Coal Tit is our smallest tit. Resident.

Identification: (11 cm). Looks like a small, insignificant version of the Great Tit; appears large-headed. The long white nape patch and striking pale cheeks are characteristic. In young birds the cheeks and nape are yellowish.

Distribution: Europe except Iceland and northern Scandinavia.

Voice: Call a high thin '*si*', '*si-si*' or '*psit*'. The song, a bright '*tsevi-tsevi-tsevi...*' or '*sitiu-sitiu-sitiu...*', can be heard almost throughout the year.

Habitat: Strongly tied to conifer woods, though quite common in deciduous woods with some conifers, as well as in suitable parks, cemeteries and gardens.

Breeding: 1–2 broods (April to June). Felty nest of moss, animal and plant wool, with spiders webs, in a hole in tree, the ground or wall. 7–11 whitish eggs, delicately speckled reddish, incubated by female; incubation 14–16 days, young fledge at 18–20 days.

Food: Insects, spiders, conifer seeds, nuts, suet.

Miscellany: May be attracted to gardens close to woodland by the provision of fairly small nestboxes with entrance hole of 26–28 mm.

Long-tailed Tit

Aegithalos caudatus

(Long-tailed Tits)

The Long-tailed Tit is unmistakable with its 'overlong' tail. Resident.

Identification: Very small body with long graduated tail (12–14 cm). Western and central European birds with broad black stripe over crown to nape, north European race with pure white head. Young with sides of head darker.

Distribution: Europe except Iceland and northern Scandinavia.

Voice: Call a thin '*tsisisi*' and a purring '*tserrr*'.

Habitat: Woodland with undergrowth, often near water. Frequent in shrubby gardens and parks.

Breeding: Single-brooded (late March to June). Very artistic domed nest with side entrance, constructed from moss, lichen, cocoons, plant and animal wool, sometimes also with shreds of paper tissues and similar. 8–12 whitish eggs, incubated by female; incubation 13–18 days, young fledge at 14–18 days.

Food: Insects and spiders.

Miscellany: Outside breeding season usually encountered in small flocks.

1. Coal Tit; 2. Long-tailed Tit; 3. Northern Long-tailed Tit; 4. Long-tailed Tit at nest

Nuthatch   *Sitta europaea*

(Nuthatches)

The Nuthatch is one of the most characteristic birds of parks and also visits gardens regularly. Resident.

Identification: Rather smaller than House Sparrow (14 cm). Stocky and powerful with strong bill and short tail. Upperparts blue-grey, underparts orange-buff, with chestnut wash on flanks, strongest on male.

Distribution: Almost the whole of Europe; missing from Iceland, Ireland and northern Scandinavia.

Voice: Has a large variety of calls; a frequent ringing *'tviet tviet tviet'* or *'tsirrr'*. Song a loud and penetrating *'vivivivivi...'* or *'tew-tew-tew-tew...'*; most of the calls can be easily imitated.

Habitat: Deciduous and mixed woodland (especially with oaks); common in parks and gardens with mature trees.

Breeding: Single-brooded (April to June). Nest of small chips of bark, mostly pine, and dry leaves – in woodpecker holes and nestboxes; in order to make larger nest sites suitable, the Nuthatch plasters up the entrance hole with wet mud so that it can only just enter. 6–9 white eggs, marked reddish-brown, incubated by female; incubation 13–16 days, young fledge at 22–25 days.

Food: Insects, spiders, seeds, nuts, suet.

Miscellany: Unlike any other of our birds the Nuthatch can climb tree trunks and branches head down as well as up. With its very powerful bill it hammers open nuts, making such a loud noise that you think a woodpecker must be the cause rather than a small bird. The Nuthatch often uses tit nestboxes, which it plasters with mud, not only around the entrance hole, but also over the front so that the lid can no longer be opened. At bird feeders in winter, which it usually visits in pairs, it dominates most other small birds.

1. The Nuthatch is a characteristic garden and parkland bird where there are mature trees; 2. It is our only bird able to climb trees head down; (Small picture on left) The nest often contains pieces of pine bark; the clutch consists of 6–9 reddish-brown speckled eggs

Short-toed Treecreeper

Certhia brachydactyla

(Treecreepers)

The Short-toed Treecreeper probes with its long curved bill in crevices in the bark of deciduous trees for insects and grubs. Resident. In Britain a rare vagrant.

Identification: Smaller than House Sparrow (12.5 cm). Upperparts the colour of bark, underparts pale with brownish flanks.

Distribution: Europe except Iceland, British Isles, northern and eastern Europe.

Voice: Call a loud high *'tiut tiut tiut'* or *'sri'*. Song a rising series of high thin whistling notes.

Habitat: Deciduous and mixed woodland; also frequent in parks and gardens with mature deciduous trees.

Breeding: 1–2 broods (April to July). Twig nest, strengthened with stalks and moss, behind loose tree bark or in nestbox; sometimes in hole in wall. 4–7 red-and-brown speckled eggs, brooded by female; incubation 13–15 days, young fledge at 16–18 days

Food: Insects and their larvae, spiders, small seeds.

Miscellany: The Short-toed Treecreeper will use specially-designed nestboxes.

Treecreeper

Certhia familiaris

(Treecreepers)

The Treecreeper is very difficult to tell apart reliably from Short-toed Treecreeper on plumage details.

Identification: Like Short-toed Treecreeper (12.5 cm), but with slightly shorter bill, longer hind claw, underparts uniformly white.

Distribution: Europe except Iceland, northern Scandinavia, and most of France and the Iberian peninsula.

Voice: Call a high quavering *'srrie'* or *'sit'*. Song phrases longer than in its close relative, consisting of two falling trills, both starting very high.

Habitat: On Continent in conifer and mixed woodland; in Britain common in deciduous woodland; also in parks and gardens.

Breeding: 1–2 broods (April to July). Twig nest in crevice behind loose tree bark or in nestbox. 4–7 eggs, spotted and speckled brownish and red, brooded by female; incubation 13–16 days, young fledge at 14–18 days.

Food: Insects and their larvae, spiders, small seeds.

Miscellany: The Treecreeper, like its Short-toed cousin, joins up with roving flocks of tits and crests outside the breeding season.

1. Short-toed Treecreeper; 2. Treecreeper; (Small picture on left) Clutch of Treecreeper

Red-backed Shrike

Lanius collurio

(Shrikes)

When food is abundant, the Red-backed Shrike makes a larder by impaling prey with its hooked bill on thorns and barbed wire. Summer visitor; May to September. In Britain no longer breeds, scarce migrant only.

Identification: Larger than House Sparrow (17 cm). Male unmistakable with its chestnut back, ash-grey head and bold black mask. Female soberly coloured with barred underparts. Young with scaly pattern above.

Distribution: Much of Europe but absent in parts of north and southwest.

Voice: Call a frequent *'dschi'* or *'trrt-trrt'*. Song a hurried warbling with much mimicry.

Habitat: Bogs and heaths with bushes, small fields with thick thorn hedges; also in parks with thorn thickets.

Breeding: Single-brooded (May to July). Nest of stalks, moss, roots and hair, low in a thorn bush. 4–6 eggs, variable in colour with darker markings on the blunt end, brooded by female; incubation 14–16 days, young fledge at 14–15 days.

Food: Large insects, lizards, small mammals and young birds.

Miscellany: Sits on tops of bushes or young trees on the lookout for prey.

Woodchat Shrike

Lanius senator

(Shrikes)

The Woodchat Shrike only lives in warmer regions. Summer visitor; April to September. In Britain very scarce visitor.

Identification: Larger than House Sparrow (18 cm). Unmistakable with its red crown and nape and white shoulder patch and rump. Female with more white on face.

Distribution: Iberian peninsula, France and Mediterranean, Poland; local in the southern part of central Europe.

Voice: When threatened a rattling *'dsche-dsche'*. Song a continuous chattering with mimicry.

Habitat: Open countryside with bushes and copses; gardens and orchards, plantations.

Breeding: Single-brooded (May to July). Solid, half-ball shaped nest of stems and fresh green plant material – especially in fruit trees, 2–6 m high. 4–6 eggs greenish to brownish, with variable markings, brooded by female; incubation 14–15 days, young fledge at 15–18 days.

Food: Large insects such as beetles, bumble-bees, honey-bees.

Miscellany: Like the Red-backed Shrike often sits on tops of bushes.

1. Male Red-backed Shrike; 2. Female Red-backed Shrike; 3. Young Red-backed Shrike; 4. Woodchat Shrike; (Small picture on left) Nest and eggs of Red-backed Shrike

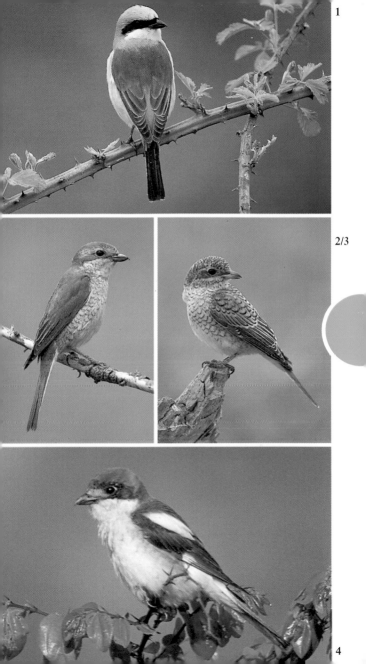

Starling

Sturnus vulgaris

(Starlings)

The Starling is one of our best-known and commonest breeding birds in parks and gardens. Partial migrant. Numbers in Britain swollen in winter by immigrants from eastern Europe.

Identification: Smaller and shorter-tailed than Blackbird (21 cm). Males identifiable in spring by their reduced pale spotting, strong violet and green plumage iridescence and pale blue base to lower mandible. Females show less iridescence, stronger pale spotting, a pale iris and pinkish base to lower mandible. In winter Starlings are heavily spotted white, the spotting wearing away, literally, as the tips of the feathers become worn towards spring, and the bill is dark in winter. Young are a dull grey-brown.

Distribution: Europe except for the Iberian peninsula, where the Starling is only a winter visitor; also extends in winter to other Mediterranean countries.

Voice: Call a penetrating *'schrien'*, alarm call a hard *'spett-spett'* or *'rrih'*. The song is very varied consisting of whistling, clicking, and chattering noises, mixed with a good deal of mimicry of both other birds and sounds.

Habitat: Deciduous and mixed woods, copses; common in parks and gardens with old trees or suitable nest sites.

Breeding: 1–2 broods a year, usually 1 in Britain (April to July). Untidy nest of stalks and leaves in tree holes, holes in walls or nestboxes. 4–7 greenish to pale blue eggs, incubated by both sexes; incubation 12–14 days, young fledge at 18–22 days.

Food: Insects, worms, snails, berries, fruit.

Miscellany: The Starling is easily recognised on the ground even from a distance by its strutting walk – quite different to the hopping gait of the Blackbird. It can easily be attracted to the garden by putting up nestboxes with 50 mm entrance hole. Outside the breeding season Starlings gather into often huge flocks and descend on vineyards and orchards in the search for ripe fruit.

1. When singing the Starling waves its wings vigorously; 2. Male in full breeding plumage; 3. Young birds are a dull grey-brown; (Small picture on left) The clutch contains 4–7 eggs with a strong bluish colour

1

2

3

Spotless Starling

Sturnus unicolor

(Starlings)

Our Starling is replaced in the Iberian Peninsula by the Spotless Starling. Resident.

Identification: The size of Starling (21 cm). In breeding plumage lacks the pale spots and green iridescence – gloss is more bluish or lilac. Covered with small white spots in non-breeding dress. Young very similar to young Starlings, but darker, almost black-brown. Behaviour like Starling, though seldom in such large flocks.

Distribution: Iberian Peninsula, southwest France, Corsica, Sardinia, Sicily, north Africa.

Voice: Song not so varied and with less mimicry than Starling.

Habitat: Like Starling.

Breeding: Often in colonies, otherwise like Starling.

Food: Insects, worms, snails, berries, fruit.

Miscellany: In Spain both species of Starlings may be seen together in winter, when the Spotless Starling appears darker because of smaller spots.

Golden Oriole

Oriolus oriolus

(Orioles)

The Golden Oriole remains well hidden in the tree canopy and, despite its dazzling plumage, is difficult to see. Summer visitor; May to September. Scarce in Britain.

Identification: A little smaller than Blackbird (24 cm). Males a magnificent yellow and black, scarcely confusable with any other species. Females and young greenish-yellow and grey.

Distribution: Europe north to southern England, southern Sweden and south Finland. Winters in Africa close to the equator.

Voice: Both sexes utter a Jay-like '*krrii*' or '*gvii*'. Song of male in spring a loud melodious whistling '*didiualiuo*'.

Habitat: Mature deciduous woodland, copses, parkland with mature trees, orchards, poplar plantations.

Breeding: Single-brooded (May to July). Elegant bowl-shaped nest of grass, stems and sometimes pieces of paper constructed by both sexes in fork of branches. 3–5 whitish or pink eggs, with a few spots, brooded by female. Incubation 16–17 days, young fledge at 16–17 days.

Food: Large insects, caterpillars, berries, fruit.

Miscellany: In flight recalls a woodpecker, with its undulating flight. It can climb well and manoeuvres acrobatically on small twigs and branches.

1. Spotless Starling; 2. Male Golden Oriole; 3. Female Golden Oriole with young; 4. Nest and eggs of Golden Oriole

Jay

(Crows)

Garrulus glandarius

With its habit of hiding acorns as a winter food-supply, the Jay might well be known as the gardener of the woods. Resident.

Identification: Smaller than Carrion Crow (34 cm). Unmistakable with its reddish-brown plumage and blue-and-black barred markings on wing.

Distribution: Europe except for Iceland and the far north of Scandinavia.

Voice: Call a loud screeching '*rrih-rrih*' or '*rretsch*' – warning other woodland birds and animals of danger; also a Buzzard-like '*hi-eh*' and a muted '*ga-hi*'. The soft chattering song with clicking and mewing noises, is very varied and ventriloquial and includes much mimicry.

Habitat: Mainly in deciduous and mixed woodland; also frequent in parks and large gardens with mature trees.

Breeding: Single-brooded (April to June). Rather small twig nest lined with grasses and lichen, usually well concealed in trees or bushes. 4–6 blue-green or olive-brown eggs, with brownish flecking and spotting, brooded by female; incubation 16–17 days, young fledge at 19–22 days.

Food: Acorns, beechmast, hazel nuts, insects; in spring also birds' eggs and young birds.

Miscellany: In flight the Jay stands out from a long way with its white rump and wing-patch. The flight is rather irregular with fluttering beats of its rounded wings. Although common it can be very difficult to actually see, as it is a shy bird and remains hidden, especially when breeding. On the Continent roams in small flocks at migration time. In autumn birds are more obvious as they fly over fields carrying acorns. In winter regularly visits feeding stations close to woodland.

1. In winter the Jay searches out the provisions it has hidden in autumn; 2. The young already show the distinctive blue and black mark on the wings; 3. These young Jays will be soon be out of the nest; (Small picture on left) The clutch contains 4–6 eggs

1

2

3

Siberian Jay

Perisoreus infaustus

1

(Crows)

The Siberian Jay is a characteristic inhabitant of the northern taiga forest, not occurring further south. Resident.

Identification: Smaller than Jay (28 cm). Unmistakable with the chestnut in its wings and tail as well as on the flanks.

Distribution: Central and northern Scandinavia, north Russia.

Voice: A variety of soft Buzzard-like and curious ringing notes.

Habitat: Northern lichen-encrusted coniferous forest.

Breeding: Single-brooded (April to May). Relatively small, well hidden nest of twigs, pieces of bark and beard-lichen, lined with feathers – usually against the trunk of a conifer. 3–4 pale greenish eggs, spotted darker, incubated by female. Incubation 19–20 days, young fledge at 21–24 days.

Food: Insects and other small creatures, eggs and young birds, berries, seeds.

Miscellany: Siberian Jays are often remarkably tame and approach man out of curiosity; they regularly visit feeders close to woodland. They investigate twigs acrobatically like tits.

Nutcracker

Nucifraga caryocatactes

2

(Crows)

The Nutcracker enjoys hazel-nuts which it sometimes comes into gardens to find in autumn. Resident. Rare irruptive vagrant to Britain.

Identification: A little smaller than Jay (32 cm). Dark brown, densely spotted white, appearing grey at a distance; wings and tail are black.

Distribution: Mountain regions of central and southeastern Europe; southern Scandinavia, northeast Europe and northern Russia.

Voice: Call a loud hoarse grating '*griirr griirr*'. Song seldom heard – a soft chattering with some mimicry.

Habitat: Conifer and mixed woods; in autumn often in gardens with hazel bushes.

Breeding: Single-brooded (March to May). Well-insulated nest of twigs, lichen, pieces of bark, earth and stems. 3–4 greenish-blue eggs with grey or olive-brown markings, incubated by both sexes; incubation 17–19 days, young fledge at 24–26 days.

Food: Seeds of Arolla pine, stone-pine and other trees, hazel-nuts and walnuts, berries, fruit.

Miscellany: Often sits on top of spruce trees. The flight action is not so irregular as Jay's. In upland regions Nutcrackers often operate a 'shuttle service' between gardens and the mountain forest carrying hazel-nuts which they hide in the forest.

1. Siberian Jay; 2. Nutcracker

1

2

Magpie

Pica pica

(Crows)

Magpies are wary birds, which nevertheless live in close proximity to man. Resident.

Identification: Smaller than Carrion Crow (44–48 cm), with very long graduated tail; unmistakable, striking black-and-white plumage.

Distribution: The whole of Europe, except Iceland.

Voice: Call a harsh chattering *'tscharr-ackackack'*, warning of danger from cats, birds of prey and man. Song a subdued chattering interspersed with nasal notes.

Habitat: Open countryside with copses and hedges, towns and villages with tall trees; in gardens, parks and cemeteries where there are trees, and even in the centre of cities.

Breeding: Single-brooded (April to May). Large dome shaped roofed nest of twigs in trees and tall bushes; the base of the nest is constructed of roots and earth. 5–8 bluish to greenish eggs, usually marked darker, brooded by female; incubation 21–22 days, young fledge at 24–30 days.

Food: Omnivorous, but especially snails, worms, insects, eggs and young birds, scraps, carrion.

Miscellany: Magpies run with a characteristic swaggering gait. In flight the birds appear somewhat hesitant with their irregular wingbeats. Where they are unpersecuted they may visit feeders in winter.

Jackdaw

Corvus monedula

(Crows)

Jackdaws remain faithful to their partner for life and the pair even search for food together. Partial migrant on Continent. Resident in Britain.

Identification: Smaller than Carrion Crow (33 cm). All black apart from grey nape and ear-coverts, pale iris. Young with brownish cast and dark iris.

Distribution: Europe except for Iceland and northern Scandinavia.

Voice: Call a short penetrating *'kya'* or *'kiack'*, a rasping *'kierr'*, and when danger threatens a high *'chiup'*. Song a series of soft chattering and mewing noises, seldom heard.

Habitat: Deciduous woodland and parks with woodpecker holes, church towers, castles, ruins and old walls.

Breeding: Single-brooded (April to June). Twig nest lined with soft plant material and animal wool; in hole in tree, crevices, holes in walls and nestboxes. 4–6 pale blue eggs with dark speckling, brooded mainly by female; incubation 17–18 days, young fledge at 28–35 days.

Food: Worms, snails, insects, fruits, mice, young birds, scraps.

Miscellany: In the evening Jackdaws flying to roost may indulge in aerobatics. Where there are cliffs the birds sail on the updraughts.

1. Magpie; 2. Young Magpies; 3. Jackdaw

Carrion/Hooded Crow

Corvus corone

(Crows)

Carrion Crows (*Corvus corone corone*) and Hooded Crows (*Corvus corone cornix*) are races of the same species. Resident.

Identification: Size 47 cm. Bill shorter and more powerful than that of the Rook, and with bristly feathers at the base covering about a third of the bill. Carrion Crows are all-black with a weak gloss. In the Hooded Crow, the back and underparts are grey, making it easy to recognise. Where the two forms meet, there is a zone of overlap in which they sometimes interbreed; the offspring are intermediate between the parents.

Distribution: Carrion Crows occur in western Europe except Ireland and northwest Scotland; they are replaced by Hooded Crows in these last two areas, as well as in eastern central Europe, eastern and northern Europe, Italy and southeast Europe.

Voice: Call a repeated *'verr'* or *'kreh'*, when mobbing birds of prey *'krrr'*. Song a soft, seldom heard, ventriloquial chattering, with mimicry of other birds.

Habitat: Open farmland, uplands, heaths; common in parks and gardens with tall trees.

Breeding: Single-brooded (March to June). Large solid nest of twigs, strengthened with mud, and lined with wool and hair, usually high in a tree fork, but also in tall bushes, on cliff ledge or buildings. 3–6 blue-green eggs, with a variety of patterning, incubated by female; incubation 17–20 days, young fledge at 31–33 days.

Food: Omnivorous: insects, worms, snails, mice, frogs, eggs and young birds, seeds, fruits, carrion, scraps.

Miscellany: Outside the breeding season both Carrion and Hooded Crows may be sociable, often joining into quite large roosting congregations, though flocks are never as large as those of the Rook.

1. In Western Europe the Carrion Crow is to be met with almost everywhere close to man; 2. The Hooded Crow replaces the Carrion Crow east of the R Elbe, as well as in northern Scotland and Ireland; (Small picture on left) Nest and eggs of Carrion Crow

1

2

Rook
Corvus frugilegus

(Crows)

The Rook is easily recognised by the whitish, unfeathered base to its bill. Resident in Britain.

Identification: The size of Carrion Crow (47 cm). Separated from this species by its steeper forehead, loose tarsus feathering ('trousers') and the blue gloss to the plumage.

Distribution: Europe except Iceland, most of Scandinavia and southwest and southern Europe. Spreads in winter across central and southern Europe, and to the Iberian peninsula.

Voice: Call similar to Carrion Crow but deeper and rougher 'kroh', 'korr', 'krah'. Chattering song, with croaking and bright, metallic notes.

Habitat: Open farmland with copses, parkland and large gardens in winter.

Breeding: Single-brooded (March to May). Colonial breeder; large nest of twigs, strengthened with stems and earth, in tops of trees. 3–6 bluish eggs with variously coloured patterning, incubated by female; incubation 16–19 days, young fledge at 29–35 days.

Food: Insects and larvae, worms, snails, mice, plant material, seeds, scraps.

Miscellany: Rooks are very gregarious all year round; in winter especially they gather into very large flocks to search for food, sometimes in parks and towns; in the evening they roost communally in tall trees.

Tree Sparrow
Passer montanus

(Sparrows)

The Tree Sparrow is a more rural species in western Europe than its relative. Resident.

Identification: A little smaller than House Sparrow (14 cm). The chestnut-brown crown, black cheek spot and white nape patch are all characteristic.

Distribution: Europe except for Iceland, most of Fennoscandia, and the western part of the Iberian peninsula.

Voice: Call a repeated 'tsvit-tek tek-tek' or 'tschick-tschick-tschock'. Song similar to the chirping of House Sparrow, but harder.

Habitat: Open farmland, villages, orchards, gardens and parks.

Breeding: 2–3 broods a year (April to August). Round nest of stems, stalks and feathers in hole in tree, wall, nestbox or artificial swallow-nest. 4–6 pale eggs with dense dark patterning, brooded by both sexes. Incubation 12–14 days, young fledge at 15–20 days.

Food: Seeds, insects, buds, fruits, scraps.

Miscellany: May visit bird tables on the edge of settlements.

1. Rooks; 2. Tree Sparrow at the nest hole; 3. Young Tree Sparrow; 4. Tree Sparrows are sociable; (Small picture on left) Nest and eggs of Rook

1

2/3

4

House Sparrow

Passer domesticus

(Sparrows)

The House Sparrow is one of the commonest birds living close to man.
Resident.

Identification: Size 15 cm. Male easily recognised by his grey crown, black
bib and pale grey underparts. In autumn not so contrasting, with pale
feather fringes on the crown and duller bib. Female much duller –
grey-brown with neat patterning and lacking the conspicuous head pattern
of the male.

Distribution: The whole of Europe except for Iceland and barren mountain
regions.

Voice: The rhythmic chirruping which everyone associates with the
Sparrow is the true song uttered by the male in the vicinity of the nest. Call
a repeated *'tschett-tschett'* or a loud penetrating chattering *'tetetetet'*.

Habitat: In close association with man and his settlements in towns, villages
and farms.

Breeding: 2–3 broods (April to August). Untidy, roofed nest of stems, stalks,
paper and other rubbish, under eaves, in holes in walls, among climbing
plants, in stork and swallow nests; occasionally free-standing nests in thick
bushes. 3–6 pale eggs, variously patterned, incubated by both sexes.
Incubation 12–14 days, young fledge at 11–19 days.

Food: Seeds, insects and their larvae, fruits, berries, grain, scraps.

Miscellany: House Sparrows can often be seen bathing in sand or dust; this
is an important part of the birds' hygiene as it helps rid them of annoying
parasites concealed in their feathers. Several males may court a female in
group display, with drooping wings and cocked tails, chirping loudly; if she
flies off she is pursued vigorously by the entire gang.

1. The male wears a black bib; 2. A young bird (left) is fed by the female; 3.
Fledged young are most easily recognised by the yellow bill flanges; (Small
picture on left) Nest with eggs

1

2

3

Chaffinch

Fringilla coelebs

(Finches)

The Chaffinch is one of the commonest birds of parks and gardens, and is to be found almost everywhere there are a few trees. Partial migrant, males and females often separating in winter.

Identification: Size of House Sparrow (15 cm). Gleaming white wingbars. Males in spring strikingly colourful with gleaming blue-grey crown, nape and bill and olive-green rump. Females rather featureless except for the white wingbars – upperparts olive-brown, underparts pale greyish-buff.

Distribution: Almost the whole of Europe except for Iceland and the far north of Scandinavia. Males do not move as far as the females in winter.

Voice: Alarm call a Great Tit-like '*pink*', in flight '*chup*'. The so-called 'rain call', a rolling '*vriut*', is not only to be heard when it is raining. Song a chattering descending phrase, with a different dialect conclusion according to geographical location. The song has been likened to the run-up and delivery of a fast bowler in cricket.

Habitat: Very common in all sorts of woodland, copses, open countryside with bushes and hedges, as well as in parks and gardens with trees, even in the middle of cities.

Breeding: Usually single-brooded (April to July). 3–6 delicate pale blue eggs with pink and brownish speckling, incubated by the female; incubation 11–13 days, young fledge at 12–14 days.

Food: Seeds, insects, spiders, fruits, berries, grain.

Miscellany: Hops along the ground with jerky head movements. Visits bird feeders in winter, especially food scattered on the ground; Chaffinches are nevertheless quite timid and are easily driven off by the threat postures of other birds. In winter they gather into large flocks, often with Bramblings or Yellowhammers in stubble or weedy fields.

1. In spring the males wear a brilliant blue-grey cap; 2. The female is rather drab except for her characteristic white wingbars; 3. Young
(Small picture on left) Nest with eggs

1

2

3

Brambling

Fringilla montifringilla

(Finches)

The Brambling is a northern species. Migrant and winter visitor, with us from October to April.

Identification: Size of Chaffinch (15.5 cm). Breast and shoulders orange, rump white. In spring males have a glossy black head and back, at other times pale feather edges make these appear scaled brownish. Females much duller with brown-patterned back.

Distribution: Scandinavia and northeast Europe. Winters in western, central and southern Europe.

Voice: Call a harsh *'queih'* and *'yek'*, in flight *'chuk'*.

Habitat: Breeds in northern forests. In winter in beech woods, fields, gardens and parks.

Breeding: Single-brooded (May to July). Nest of moss, stalks, lichen and feathers, usually in a fork. 5–7 pale bluish eggs marked with rusty, incubated by the female; incubation 11–12 days, young fledge at 12–14 days.

Food: Insects, beechmast and other seeds.

Miscellany: In winter in large flocks in beech woods; also at bird feeders.

Hawfinch

Coccothraustes coccothraustes

(Finches)

The Hawfinch is quite unmistakable with its bright plumage and huge bill. Resident.

Identification: Larger than House Sparrow (18 cm). Stocky and short-tailed. In spring and summer bill blue-grey, in winter yellowish-horn. Male very bright, female a little duller.

Distribution: Europe except for Iceland, Ireland and the north.

Voice: Call a short, sharp *'tsicks'* or *'tsittit'*. Song: a series of call-like nasal notes, seldom heard.

Habitat: Deciduous and mixed woods, parks and gardens, with mature deciduous trees.

Breeding: Single-brooded (April to June). Large nest of twigs, stalks and small roots, high in a deciduous tree. 4–6 bluish-grey eggs with dark brown markings; incubation 11–13 days, young fledge at 11–14 days.

Food: Seeds of deciduous trees, especially hornbeam and maple.

Miscellany: On the Continent often at bird-tables in winter in flocks; with their huge bills, they avoid competition from other birds.

1. Male Brambling in late winter; 2. Female Brambling in winter; 3. Male Hawfinch in winter; 4. Male Hawfinch when breeding; (Small picture on left) Nest and eggs of Hawfinch

Serin

Serinus serinus

(Finches)

The Serin is our smallest finch. Summer visitor; March to October. Scarce visitor to Britain.

Identification: Distinctly smaller than House Sparrow (11.5 cm). Males canary-yellow, streaked brownish on back and flanks. Females more grey-green and much more strongly streaked.

Distribution: Southern, southwest and central Europe, north Africa.

Voice: Call a trilling '*girr*' or '*girlitt*'. Song a high continuous tinkling; often sings from high songpost such as TV aerial or in song flight.

Habitat: Around settlements: in parks and gardens, cemeteries, and in open deciduous and mixed woodland.

Breeding: Double-brooded (April to July). Small neat nest of stems, roots, moss, feathers, hair and plant wool, usually in young conifer or bush. 3–5 greenish or bluish eggs speckled reddish and pale lilac; incubated by the female; incubation 12–14 days, young fledge at 14–16 days.

Food: Small seeds, green plant material, insects.

Miscellany: In spring the males display in bat-like song-flights.

Siskin

Carduelis spinus

(Finches)

The Siskin is one of our smallest finches. Partial migrant.

Identification: Smaller than House Sparrow (12 cm). The slim, pointed bill and greenish-yellow plumage are characteristic. Males have a black cap and chin. Females are more grey-green, lacking black on the head, and are more strongly streaked.

Distribution: British Isles, north, northeast and central Europe, parts of southeast Europe.

Voice: Call a repeated '*tettettett*', in flight '*tsiiuh*' or '*tiuuli*'. Song a lively urgent twittering with a squeezed, drawn-out ending.

Habitat: Mainly in upland conifer woods, but also in extensive forests; wanders widely in the lowlands in winter.

Breeding: Double-brooded (April to July). Neat nest of small twigs, stems, moss and lichen, usually high in a conifer. 4–6 delicate pale blue eggs with fine reddish and violet spotting, incubated by the female; incubation 12–13 days, young fledge at 13–15 days.

Food: Seeds of trees and weeds, insects.

Miscellany: In winter flocks of Siskins can often be found feeding acrobatically on birches and alders. Especially in late winter they come to bird feeders in parks and gardens.

1. Male Serin; 2. Female Serin; 3. Female Siskin; 4. Male Siskin

Greenfinch

Carduelis chloris

(Finches)

The Greenfinch is the largest yellow-green European finch, and one of the commonest birds in our parks and gardens. Resident.

Identification: Size of House Sparrow (15 cm). The stocky body, powerful cone-shaped bill and yellow marks on the wings and tail are conspicuous. Male yellow-green, female much duller, more grey-green. In autumn and winter both sexes are less brightly coloured. Young browner, heavily streaked darker.

Distribution: Europe except for Iceland and parts of northern Scandinavia and northeast Europe.

Voice: Call a repeated ringing *'giugiugiu'*, when alarmed a nasal drawn-out *'djiui'*, when arguing a grating *'tsrrr'*. Song musical with rich canary-like trilling and ringing phrases, with whistling notes recalling Nuthatch. Regularly performs a bat-like song flight with strong, slow, rowing wingbeats.

Habitat: Open woodland and woodland edge; farmland with copses, hedges, orchards and avenues of trees; villages and towns where there are trees, especially in parks and gardens.

Breeding: 2–3 broods a year (April to August). Large nest of twigs, moss, roots, stems and plant wool, usually not very high in young trees, bushes or in climbers against a house wall. 4–6 whitish eggs with brownish and blackish speckling, incubated by the female; incubation 12–15 days, young fledge at 13–16 days.

Food: Various seeds, flower buds, insects, sunflower seeds, nuts.

Miscellany: Greenfinches are often the commonest visitor to bird feeders in gardens and parks. They are generally quarrelsome and fiercely threaten other birds, with wings raised and slightly apart, tail fanned and bill wide open. The yellow markings in wing and tail reinforce the visual threat signal.

1. Male showing the striking yellow patch in wing; 2. The female is much duller; 3. Young in the nest; (Small picture on left) Nest with eggs

1

2

3

Goldfinch

Carduelis carduelis

(Finches)

The Goldfinch is one of our prettiest birds. Partial migrant.

Identification: Smaller than House Sparrow (13 cm). With its bright colour scheme, unmistakable; the characteristic black, white and red head markings are not attained by the young until October.

Distribution: Europe except for Iceland and much of the north.

Voice: Call an almost continuous bright tinkling '*steeglit*' or '*didlit*', when arguing a grating '*tschrr*', alarm call a nasal '*dvi-ii*'.

Habitat: Orchards, villages with tall deciduous trees, parks and gardens where there are deciduous trees. In winter more in open countryside.

Breeding: Double-brooded (May to August). Carefully constructed thick-walled nest of plant wool, stems and moss, usually quite high in trees and bushes. 4–6 reddish-patterned eggs, incubated by the female; incubation 12–13 days, young fledge at 14–15 days.

Food: Seeds, buds, insects.

Miscellany: Goldfinches are most often seen in flocks along road verges or in weedy fields, where they extract the seeds of thistles and other plants with their pointed bills.

Redpoll

Carduelis flammea

(Finches)

The Redpoll is a regular garden visitor where there are birch trees. Partial migrant.

Identification: Smaller than House Sparrow (13 cm). Grey-brown with red crown and black chin. In breeding plumage males also show an intense red flush on the breast.

Distribution: Iceland, British Isles, north and central Europe.

Voice: Flight call a rapid nasal '*dschedschedsche*'. Song a hoarse twittering and trilling with flight calls included.

Habitat: Open conifer woods in upland regions; in lowlands, parks and gardens.

Breeding: Double-brooded (May to July). Small nest of twigs, moss and stems in conifers or scrub. 4–6 pale blue eggs with reddish and brownish markings, incubated by the female; incubation 11–13 days, young fledge at 11–14 days.

Food: Seeds of deciduous trees and weeds, insects.

Miscellany: In winter Redpolls are often seen in flocks on birches and alders.

1. Goldfinch; 2. Pair of Redpolls, female on left, male on right; (Small picture on left) Nest and eggs of Goldfinch

Bullfinch

Pyrrhula pyrrhula

(Finches)

The Bullfinch is one of our most attractive birds. Unlike other small birds, pairs remain faithful, and several couples may join together into small parties. Partial migrant.

Identification: Only a little larger than House Sparrow (16 cm), but appears much plumper. The black cap, black bill, black tail and white rump, which is striking in flight, are all characteristic. Males have bright rose-red, female pinkish-grey underparts. Young similar to female, but lacking black cap.

Distribution: Europe except for Iceland, parts of northern Europe and the Iberian peninsula.

Voice: Call a soft melancholy piping *'diuu'* or *'viup'*. The inconspicuous piping song with its creaking and squeezed notes appears ventriloquial. Hand-reared Bullfinches learn to imitate songs and tunes.

Habitat: Conifer and mixed woods, copses, large hedges; common in gardens, orchards, cemeteries and parks.

Breeding: Double-brooded (May to August). Well-hidden, loosely constructed nest of twigs, roots and moss in thick bushes and conifers. 4–6 pale blue eggs with violet and blackish markings, incubated by the female; incubation 12–14 days, young fledge at 14–16 days.

Food: Seeds of trees and weeds, buds, berries, insects, sunflower seeds, nuts, grain.

Miscellany: During the breeding season Bullfinches remain concealed and are difficult to see. When feeding, usually in pairs or small groups, their colourful pattern gives them away. Unlike the other larger finches they seldom squabble, and hardly ever associate with other birds – possibly because with their preference for buds they do not come to bird-feeders.

1. The male has rose-red underparts; 2. The female has pinkish-grey underparts; 3. Both adults feed the young, often together; (Small picture on left) Nest containing the pale blue eggs marked with violet and blackish markings

1

2

3

Linnet

Carduelis cannabina

(Finches)

The Linnet is a characteristic small bird of gardens, cemeteries and open parks. Partial migrant.

Identification: A little smaller than House Sparrow (13.5 cm). In spring males are red on the head, breast and rump, with the back red-brown. Female and young streaked, lacking red.

Distribution: Europe except for Iceland and northern Scandinavia.

Voice: Call a rather stuttering nasal *'gegegegeg'*. Song rich and melodious, with twittering, trilling, warbling and chattering notes.

Habitat: Open farmland with hedges and copses, vineyards; common in cemeteries, gardens and parks.

Breeding: Double-brooded (April to August). Nest of stems, roots and plant fibres, usually low in hedges, bushes or young trees; several pairs often nest close together. 4–6 whitish eggs with reddish or violet flecking, incubated almost entirely by the female; incubation 11–13 days, young fledge at 11–16 days.

Food: Seeds of weeds and trees, insects.

Miscellany: Rather wary. Outside the breeding season Linnets are found in open country where they seek weed seeds.

Common Rosefinch

Carpodacus erythrinus

(Finches)

The Rosefinch is an eastern species, which is currently spreading westwards. Summer visitor; May to September. Scarce visitor to Britain, has bred recently.

Identification: A little smaller than House Sparrow (14.5 cm). Old males have red head, breast and rump. Female and young males lack red.

Distribution: North and east Europe, central Europe, spreading west.

Voice: Call *'tslit-tslit'* and a soft *'tschiui'*. Song a short, oriole-like whistling phrase *'diu-diu-di-diuidyu'*.

Habitat: Damp habitats with willows, birch and alders, scrubby countryside, parkland, gardens.

Breeding: Single-brooded (May to July). Loosely made nest of stems, small roots and hair, usually low in a thick bush. 4–6 pale blue eggs with dark markings. Incubation 11–12 days, young fledge at 10–13 days.

Food: Buds, catkins, seeds, insects.

Miscellany: The end of May and June is the best time to listen out for singing Rosefinches.

1. Male Linnet; 2. Female Linnet; 3. Female Common Rosefinch feeding young; 4. Male Common Rosefinch; (Small picture on left) Nest and eggs of Linnet

1

2/3

4

Pine Grosbeak

Pinicola enucleator

(Finches)

The Pine Grosbeak is a large northern finch, which visits parks and gardens in Scandinavia in winter. Partial migrant. Very rare vagrant to Britain.

Identification: Much bigger than House Sparrow (19 cm). Hooked bill, two white wingbars. Males carmine-red, females yellow-brown.

Distribution: The taiga forest of central and northern Scandinavia, north Finland and north Russia.

Voice: Call *'byiit byiit'* and a clear *'tiudli-liuh'*. Falling song of clear hollow notes.

Habitat: Open woodland with ground layer of bilberry and cranberry. In winter favours rowan.

Breeding: Single-brooded (May to July). Loosely woven nest of thin twigs, stems and lichen, low in a conifer. 3–4 eggs, brooded by the female; incubation 13–14 days, young fledge at 13–16 days.

Food: Seeds, buds, insects, berries.

Miscellany: Pine Grosbeaks come from remote breeding grounds and in winter are often remarkably confiding; they may even appear in the middle of towns on rowan trees.

Crossbill

Loxia curvirostra

(Finches)

Crossbills are restless birds, which wander far and wide throughout the year in search of ripe cones. Partial migrant.

Identification: Larger and more powerfully built than House Sparrow (17 cm). The upper and lower mandibles are crossed at the tip. Male brick-red, female olive-green. The brownish young are heavily streaked.

Distribution: Conifer woods right across Europe, but with large gaps.

Voice: Flight call a penetrating *'kipp kipp'*. Song of hoarse twittering and jangling phrases, mixed with flight calls. Sings almost throughout the year.

Habitat: Chiefly spruce woods, from the lowlands right up to the tree-line; also in parks and large gardens with mature spruce trees.

Breeding: 1–2 broods a year (at any time of the year, though mostly January to May). Solid nest of twigs, stems, moss and lichen, usually high in a spruce tree. 3–4 greenish or pale bluish eggs with lilac and brown speckling, incubated by the female; incubation 14–16 days, young fledge at 20–25 days.

Food: Conifer seeds, especially those of spruce; insects.

Miscellany: Crossbills are very sociable and are usually seen in flocks; they are most easily found by their penetrating flight calls.

1. Male Pine Grosbeak; 2. Male Crossbill tackling a cone

1

2

Yellowhammer

Emberiza citrinella

(Buntings)

In open countryside the Yellowhammer is often one of the commonest birds. Partial migrant.

Identification: A little bigger, slimmer and longer-tailed than House Sparrow (16.5 cm). An important field mark is the cinnamon-brown rump, and in flight also the white outer tail feathers. Males with head and underparts bright lemon-yellow; when breeding females have less yellow and more strongly streaked underparts, while in their first winter they are olive-brown and lack yellow.

Distribution: The whole of Europe except for Iceland and most of the Iberian peninsula.

Voice: Call a repeated 'tsrik', 'tsiu' or 'tsiurr'. Song a simple, rather melancholy, ringing phrase, beginning with higher notes and falling 'zizizizizizie-diuh'.

Habitat: Fields with clumps of bushes, copses and hedges, woodland edge, young conifer plantations; quite frequent at the edge of villages, in large gardens and parkland.

Breeding: Double-brooded (April to July). Well-hidden, cup-shaped nest of stems, moss, leaves and fine plant material, usually in a low bush, close to the ground, among tall grasses; many nests are built on banks. 3–5 whitish eggs, covered with irregular grey and dark reddish scribbling, normally incubated by the female; incubation 12–14 days, young fledge at 11–14 days.

Food: Seeds, buds, insects, spiders, grain.

Miscellany: In high summer, the Yellowhammer is often the only bird still tirelessly singing in the heat of the day; the males usually sing from an elevated perch at the top of a bush or electric cable. In winter Yellowhammers regularly come to the edge of settlements and farmyards, where they search for food on the ground; they are sometimes to be found in company with finches and Tree Sparrows where scraps are put out for the birds. The related Reed Bunting regularly visits gardens for food in winter.

1. The male often sings on into high summer; the diagnostic cinnamon rump is clearly visible; 2. Females are distinctly streaked; 3. Young Yellowhammers soon after leaving the nest; (Small picture on left) The eggs are covered with irregular scribbles

1

2

3

1 Ortolan Bunting

Emberiza hortulana

(Buntings)

The Ortolan is a decreasing species which prefers warm lowlands. Summer visitor; April to October. Scarce migrant only in Britain.

Identification: Size of Yellowhammer (16.5 cm). Best separated from this species by its grey head and sulphur-yellow eyering and moustachial stripe. Females less brightly coloured, underparts with some streaking.

Distribution: Europe except for Iceland, the British Isles, parts of northern and northwestern Europe, including the British Isles, and parts of the Iberian peninsula. Winters in Africa south of the Sahara.

Voice: Call a repeated *'psie'* or short *'tiup'*. Song a rather melancholy phrase *'tsri-tsri-tsri-tsri-driu-driu-driu'*.

Habitat: Varied farmland with copses, rows of trees or even just a single tree, usually on a slope and often near damp ground; orchards and open parkland.

Breeding: Single-brooded (May to July). Nest of dry stalks, grass stems, roots and animal hair – mostly on the ground under bushes, well hidden in the vegetation. 4–6 pale pink eggs with dark speckles and lines, incubated by the female; incubation 11–13 days, young fledge at 12–13 days.

Food: Seeds, green plant material, insects.

Miscellany: Ortolans are shy and easily disturbed. Outside the breeding season usually in small groups.

2 Cirl Bunting

Emberiza cirlus

(Buntings)

The Cirl Bunting prefers warmer regions and is now confined in Britain to Devon, where resident.

Identification: Size of Yellowhammer, but appears plumper (16.5 cm). Males easily identified with their black and yellow striped head and black throat, females very similar to female Yellowhammer, but with less yellow in plumage and olive-brown, rather than cinnamon, rump.

Distribution: Iberian peninsula north to southwest England, northern France and western part of central Europe; south and southeast Europe, north Africa.

Voice: Call a high *'tsieh'* or sharp *'tsip'*. The song recalls that of Lesser Whitethroat – a monotonous rattling *'tzi-tzetzetzetzetze'*.

Habitat: Open countryside with isolated trees and bushes, usually on sunny slopes, in vineyards and orchards, in parks and gardens at the edges of villages.

Breeding: Double-brooded (May to August). Nest of stems, moss, fibres, roots and animal hair, well-hidden in ground vegetation, often under a bush or against a low wall. 3–5 whitish to pale lilac eggs with dark brown speckles and squiggles, incubated by the female; incubation 12–13 days, young fledge at 11–13 days.

Food: Seeds, insects.

Miscellany: Despite the striking plumage of the male, Cirl Buntings are unobtrusive birds, difficult to find; they are best located by their song.

1. Male Ortolan; 2. Male Cirl Bunting

1 Swift

Apus apus

(Swifts)

With their shrill calls and sickle-winged silhouette Swifts are a familiar feature of the summer sky. Summer visitor; May to August.

Identification: Larger than Swallow (16.5 cm). All black plumage, paler only on the chin and throat. With their pale feather fringes young appear scaly.

Distribution: The whole of Europe except for Iceland and parts of northern Europe. Winters in tropical Africa.

Voice: Call a loud piercing *'srieh'*.

Habitat: Over towns, villages and the open countryside.

Breeding: Single-brooded (May to August). Shallow cup-shaped nest of stems, leaves and feathers gathered in flight, stuck together with saliva, usually in a dark cavity under the eaves, in hole in wall or special nestbox. 2–3 elongated white eggs, incubated by both sexes; incubation 18–25 days, young fledge at 5–7 weeks.

Food: Flying insects and ballooning spiders.

Miscellany: Only exceptionally found on the ground. Small parties often fly at high speed around the rooftops, screaming.

2 Kingfisher

Alcedo atthis

(Kingfishers)

The Kingfisher is our most colourful small bird, and easily recognised. Partial migrant.

Identification: Not much bigger than House Sparrow (16.5 cm). Turquoise-blue and orange-chestnut coloration and short tail. Female with reddish base to lower mandible of otherwise all-black bill.

Distribution: Europe as far north as Scotland, southern Sweden and southern Finland.

Voice: Call a penetrating *'tsiiiiit'*. Song consists of variations on the call and bright trilling notes.

Habitat: Clear streams and rivers, with fringing vegetation and steep banks to provide suitable nest sites. Outside the breeding season on all sorts of water bodies including park lakes.

Breeding: 2–3 broods a year (April to August). Excavates a horizontal tunnel up to a metre long with an enlarged nest chamber at the end. 5–7 white eggs, incubated by both sexes; incubation 19–21 days, young fledge at 23–27 days.

Food: Small fish, larvae of aquatic insects.

Miscellany: The Kingfisher often sits motionless on a perch over the water on the lookout for fish swimming below; when it flies off, it usually utters its penetrating call.

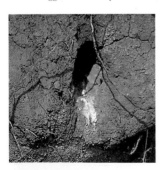

1. Swift; 2. Female Kingfisher; (Small picture on left) Kingfisher nest-hole

1

2

Hoopoe

Upupa epops

(Hoopoes)

The Hoopoe is a characteristic bird of southern European orchards, parks and olive groves. Summer visitor; April to September. In Britain very scarce migrant, has bred.

Identification: Size of Blackbird (27 cm). Richly coloured with orange-brown body feathers and black-and-white patterned wings and tail; erectile black-tipped fan crest.

Distribution: Europe north to northern France, and Estonia in the east, but uncommon in the north of its range. Winters in southern Spain and Africa.

Voice: The territorial song is a muffled, far-carrying hooting *'up-up-up'*.

Habitat: Open woodland with mature trees, bare ground, gardens, vineyards, olive groves, orchards and parkland.

Breeding: Single-brooded (May to July). Nests in holes in tree trunk or branch, walls, stone piles and in large nestboxes. 5–8 pale grey eggs, incubated by female; incubation 15–17 days, young fledge at 26–29 days.

Food: Large insects and their larvae, often extracted from dung heaps.

Miscellany: The Hoopoe is a striking bird in flight with its black-and-white wing- and tail-pattern, recalling a large butterfly; on the ground it often crouches low and is then difficult to find.

Wryneck

Jynx torquilla

(Woodpeckers)

The Wryneck is a woodpecker which looks more like a songbird. Summer visitor; April to September. Rare in Britain, now usually only a migrant.

Identification: Smaller than Blackbird (16.5 cm), with a short songbird-like bill. Bark-coloured plumage; flight undulating, with long glides.

Distribution: Europe except for Iceland, the British Isles and parts of the Iberian peninsula. Winters in tropical Africa.

Voice: Call an occasional hissing *'gschrih'* or *'teck-teck-teck'*. Song a crescendo series of pitiful ringing notes *'gyegyegyegye...'*.

Habitat: Open deciduous woodland, orchards, cemeteries, parks and large gardens with old deciduous trees.

Breeding: 1–2 broods a year (May to August). 6–10 white eggs, which are laid in a tree hole without nest material, and incubated by both sexes; incubation 12–14 days, young fledge at 18–22 days.

Food: Mainly ant pupae, but also other insects.

Miscellany: The Wryneck is a very retiring bird, and its cryptic plumage makes it difficult to find. This scarce visitor can be aided by the provision of nestboxes (entrance hole 46–50 mm).

1. When excited the Hoopoe raises its crest, 2 Adult at the nest-hole; 3. Wryneck at the nest-hole; 4. Wryneck

1

2/3

4

Green Woodpecker   *Picus viridis*
(Woodpeckers)

The Green Woodpecker reveals its presence by its loud yaffling call, rather than by drumming. Resident.

Identification: Much bigger than Blackbird (32 cm). Upperparts green with red crown and bright yellow rump. Male with red moustachial stripe edged black, that of female all black. Young barred.

Distribution: Europe except for Iceland, Ireland, much of northern Europe.

Voice: Call in flight '*kiu-kiu-kiuck*'. Territorial song is a '*gliu-gliu-gliu…*'.

Habitat: Deciduous woodland, copses, orchards, avenues, parkland, and large gardens with mature trees.

Breeding: Single-brooded (April to July). Nests in self-excavated or, more often, in appropriated hole. 5–8 white eggs, incubated by both sexes; incubation 15–19 days, young fledge at 23–27 days.

Food: Ants and their pupae, other insects, worms, snails, fruit.

Miscellany: In winter Green Woodpeckers even dig through the snow to ant-hills. Rarely visits bird-tables.

Grey-headed Woodpecker   *Picus canus*
(Woodpeckers)

Grey-headed Woodpeckers remain secretive, especially at the start of the nesting period. Presence is often noted only by territorial song and drumming (of about two seconds duration). Resident. Not recorded in Britain.

Identification: Larger than Blackbird (26 cm). Upperparts greenish-yellow with yellow rump, head and neck grey; plumage altogether greyer than Green Woodpecker. Male with bright red forecrown and black moustachial stripe; female lacking red.

Distribution: Europe except for Iceland, most of northern Europe, British Isles, the Iberian and Italian peninsulas and northern central Europe.

Voice: Call a rather hoarse '*kiu*' or a squeezed '*kiuuk*'. Territorial song is a far-carrying falling series of rather pitiful ringing '*giu*' notes, easily imitated.

Habitat: Deciduous and mixed woodland; orchards, parks and cemeteries.

Breeding: Single-brooded (April to July). Excavates its own nest hole or uses an available woodpecker hole. 7–9 white eggs, incubated by both sexes; incubation 15–17 days, young fledge at 24–25 days.

Food: Chiefly ants and ant pupae, other insects, berries, fruit, seeds. Seeks food mostly on ground.

Miscellany: In winter the Grey-headed Woodpecker regularly visits bird feeders.

1. Male Green Woodpecker; 2. Male Grey-headed Woodpecker; 3. Female Grey-headed Woodpecker; 4. Female Green Woodpecker; (Small picture on left) Male Green Woodpecker at the nest-hole

Great Spotted Woodpecker   *Dendrocopos major*

(Woodpeckers)

The Great Spotted Woodpecker is our commonest woodpecker, and in many places a familiar sight in parks and gardens. Resident.

Identification: Smaller than Blackbird (23 cm). Black, white and red woodpecker with striking white shoulder patches and bright red undertail coverts. Male with red patch on nape. Young with red crown, paler pinky-red under tail.

Distribution: Almost the whole of Europe except for Iceland, Ireland and the far north.

Voice: Call a frequent metallic '*kick*', repeated rapidly when alarmed. In spring courtship a hoarse '*ri-ri...*' as the birds pursue each other through the tree canopy.

Habitat: All types of woodland, though especially favours oak and hornbeam; common in parks and gardens with tall trees, even in the middle of cities.

Breeding: Single-brooded (May to June). Great Spotted Woodpeckers excavate a new nest hole every year and therefore create potential nest sites for other hole-nesting birds and mammals. 4–7 white eggs, incubated by both sexes; incubation 10–13 days, young fledge at 20–24 days.

Food: Wood-dwelling insects and their larvae, especially beetles and moths; tree sap; eggs and young of other birds taken from nestboxes which are chiselled open. In winter mainly conifer seeds, nuts and fat.

Miscellany: The characteristic drumming has the same function as song, to proclaim territory, and is therefore a good identification feature. The drumming of the Great Spotted Woodpecker is relatively short, lasting about half a second, each blow accelerating. Nuts wedged in bark crevices are also a good indication of the species' presence. The bird often enlarges available cracks with purposeful blows of its bill to make them the right size to hold cones and nuts, which can then be dealt with in this 'woodpecker anvil'.

1. Female lacking red on the head; 2. Young with red crown; (Small picture on left) Male (with red nape) dealing with a cone at a 'woodpecker anvil'

1 Middle Spotted Woodpecker

(Woodpeckers) *Dendrocopos medius*

A characteristic bird of parkland with old oaks. Resident. Not recorded in Britain.

Identification: Rather smaller than Great Spotted Woodpecker (22 cm), with smaller bill, complete red crown, pink undertail, distinctly streaked underparts and lacking black moustache.

Distribution: North Spain, France, central, east and southeast Europe. Locally distributed.

Voice: Call a soft '*kiuk*'. A squawking '*quiii-quiii-quiii-quiii*' may be given at any time of the year.

Habitat: Ancient lowland deciduous woodland with oaks and hornbeams, in copses, orchards and parkland.

Breeding: Single-brooded (May to July). Excavates own nest-hole in rotten stump or large branch. 5–6 white eggs, incubated by both sexes; incubation 11–14 days, young fledge at 22–23 days.

Food: Various insects, nuts, seeds, fat.

Miscellany: The Middle Spotted Woodpecker probes in bark and crevices for insects or gleans prey from twigs.

2 Lesser Spotted Woodpecker *Dendrocopos minor*

(Woodpeckers)

The Lesser Spotted Woodpecker is our smallest woodpecker. Resident.

Identification: Size of House Sparrow (14.5 cm), with small bill. Male with black-bordered red crown; female totally lacking red.

Distribution: Europe except for Iceland, Ireland, Scotland and most of the Iberian peninsula.

Voice: In spring a frequent Kestrel-like '*ki-ki-ki-ki-ki...*'.

Habitat: Deciduous and mixed woods and copses with mature trees, parkland with old willows, orchards.

Breeding: Single-brooded (May to July). Excavates own hole in rotten stump or branch. 4–6 white eggs, incubated by both sexes; incubation 11–12 days, young fledge at 19–21 days.

Food: Insects on twigs and under bark; sunflower seeds.

Miscellany: Both male and female drum in the spring, drumming extended, 1–2 seconds long, on a dry branch. Sounds weaker than Great Spotted

Woodpecker and is often repeated after a short interval. The Lesser Spotted Woodpecker occasionally visits bird feeders.

1. Middle Spotted Woodpecker; 2. Male Lesser Spotted Woodpecker; (Small picture on left) Female Lesser Spotted Woodpecker at nest hole

Cuckoo

Cuculus canorus

(Cuckoos)

The Cuckoo is one of our best known birds, as it has an easily remembered call, and occurs in all types of countryside. Summer visitor; May to September.

Identification: Smaller than Feral Pigeon (33 cm). With its grey upperparts and cross-barred underparts, the plumage pattern recalls that of Sparrowhawk, though Cuckoos have pointed wings. Females have a distinct breast-band. A rare plumage variant in females is rufous, with the entire body banded. Like this rare morph, young are barred all over, but are more brown or slate-grey, with a white nape patch, and the upperparts appear 'scaly' with their pale feather edges.

Distribution: The whole of Europe except for Iceland; northwest Africa. Winters in Africa south of the Sahara.

Voice: During the breeding season the female utters a loud bubbling trill. The territorial song of the male is the well-known *'kuck-kuh kuck-kuh...'* or, when excited, *'kuckuck-kuu'*.

Habitat: Occurs in almost all natural habitats except dense woodland. Prefers semi-open varied habitat with good songposts; also to be found in parkland.

Breeding: May to July. Each female specialises in a specific host and always lays eggs of the same type; she lays up to 20 (but more usually from 9–11) eggs singly, each in a different nest. Incubation by host bird 11–13 days, young fledge at 19 days. Regular hosts include Meadow Pipit, Dunnock, Reed Warbler, Pied Wagtail, Redstart and Black Redstart, Garden Warbler and Robin, though only the first three in Britain.

Food: Mainly hairy caterpillars, though also other insects such as grasshoppers and beetles.

Miscellany: The Cuckoo is most often seen in flight, with its falcon-like silhouette, the shallow wingbeats appearing weak.

1. The Cuckoo's plumage recalls that of the Sparrowhawk; 2. After fledging the young Cuckoo draws attention to itself with its loud begging calls; 3. Reed Warblers are favourite foster parents of young Cuckoos; (Small picture on left) Nest and eggs of a Garden Warbler containing a Cuckoo's egg

Barn Owl

Tyto alba

(Barn Owls)

Barn Owls are active mainly at night and spend the day hiding in a dark corner. Resident.

Identification: About the size of a Feral Pigeon (35 cm). Strikingly pale and long-legged, and with a large heart-shaped facial disc and relatively small black eyes. Upperparts golden brown; underparts white to yellowish white – either unmarked or with dark tear-shaped spots.

Distribution: Europe except for Iceland, Scandinavia and northeast and much of eastern Europe. Rather patchy distribution within its large range.

Voice: At the start of the breeding season both male and female utter shrieking and snoring noises. Territorial song of the male is a hoarse quavering hiss *'khriuhriuhriu...'* lasting for about 2 seconds.

Habitat: Varied open farmland near human settlement. Hunts along open corridors, such as paths or verges. Widely distributed, but local.

Breeding: 1 or 2 broods per year (April to September). Nests in holes in roof spaces, church towers, barns and similar buildings, which are safe from disturbance. 4–7 white eggs, incubated by female; incubation 30–34 days, young fledge at around two months.

Food: Voles, field mice, also shrews when there is a vole-shortage; occasionally also birds, frogs, insects.

Miscellany: Barn Owls will successfully move into quiet buildings in suitable farmland habitat where nestboxes are provided. In severe winters the population suffers large losses; the birds can be helped effectively by leaving barns and other uninhabited buildings open so that they can catch mice inside. Rodents are easily attracted by scattering waste grain!

1. Barn Owls often hunt in barns where there are plenty of mice to prey on;
2. An adult returns with a field vole it has just caught; (Small picture on left) The eggs are laid in a dark corner

1

2

Tawny Owl

Strix aluco

(Owls)

The Tawny Owl is our largest owl and is known to most people with its blood-curdling calls, which are often used in horror films to produce a spooky atmosphere. Resident.

Identification: Larger than Feral Pigeon (38 cm). A powerful, stocky owl with large head and large black eyes. Bark-coloured plumage pattern on a grey or (less often) brown ground colour. In flight the broad rounded wings, which are barred underneath, and the large round head are characteristic.

Distribution: Europe except for Iceland, Ireland and most of northern Europe.

Voice: Female call a soft repeated '*kiu-itt*'. The territorial song of the male is heard as early as autumn, a spine-chilling tremulous ringing '*huuoh hu-hu-hu-huuh*'.

Habitat: Deciduous and mixed woods, not too dense, and with at least a few old trees; common in parks and large gardens with mature trees, even in the middle of towns.

Breeding: Single-brooded (February to June). Nests in large tree hole, or in old crow or bird of prey nest; also in dark, quiet corners of buildings and in large nestboxes. 2–5 white eggs, incubated by the female; incubation 28–30 days, young leave nest at 25–30 days, fledge a week later.

Food: The most catholic of our owls in its choice of prey: mice and voles, rats, shrews, birds, frogs, toads, fish, large insects.

Miscellany: The otherwise strictly nocturnal Tawny Owl often sits outside its nest-hole throughout the day in fine weather to sun itself; not infrequently small birds come across the 'enemy' and reveal the owl with their scolding alarm calls. When the owl is breeding, its nest site should never be approached too closely as at that time the owls are very aggressive and occasionally strike humans; the late Eric Hosking, the famous bird-photographer, lost an eye in a Tawny Owl attack. When there are no suitable tree holes, Tawny Owls will readily take to large nestboxes; they should only be encouraged where smaller owls, such as Little Owl (and on the Continent, Tengmalm's and Pygmy Owls) are not at risk, as they will readily take the smaller species as prey.

1. The Tawny Owl has a rounded head and striking large black eyes; 2. At first the young wear a coat of white down; (Small picture on left) Young in brown juvenile plumage

1

2

Long-eared Owl
Asio otus

(Owls)

Long-eared Owls remain well hidden in trees during the day, usually close to the trunk, so they are very difficult to find. Resident.

Identification: About same size as Feral Pigeon (36 cm). Plumage colour of bark; long feather 'ears'; orange-yellow eyes.

Distribution: Europe except for Iceland and much of northern Europe; in winter only in much of the Iberian peninsula and southern Italy.

Voice: Alarm call a barking *'uek'*. The male's courtship song is a rather soft, muffled *'huh'*. Young birds betray their presence with a plaintive, rather tremulous creaking *'stsieh'*.

Habitat: Copses, woodland edge, avenues, parks and cemeteries.

Breeding: Single-brooded (March to June). Usually uses old nest of crow or Magpie, sometimes also pigeon or bird of prey nests. 3–6 eggs, incubated by female; incubation 27–28 days, young leave nest at 21–24 days, fledge from 30 days.

Food: Field mice, voles, small birds.

Miscellany: In winter Long-eared Owls may be met with in parks and large gardens, sometimes even in built-up areas; up to a dozen or more birds may roost together in trees or bushes during the day.

Scops Owl
Otus scops

(Owls)

The monotonous repeated *'diu'* of the Scops Owl is a familiar night-time sound in gardens and parks in southern Europe. Summer visitor, April to September. Rare vagrant to Britain.

Identification: Smaller than Blackbird (19 cm). Bark-coloured, finely streaked cryptic grey plumage, with often conspicuous feather 'ears'.

Distribution: Southern Europe to northern France, parts of eastern Europe.

Voice: Territorial song is a single pure note, *'diu'*, repeated at regular intervals.

Habitat: Farmland with copses, olive groves, orchards, woodland edge; large gardens and parks.

Breeding: Single-brooded (May to July). Nests in tree hole, crevice in wall or cliff, or in nestbox. 3–6 white eggs, incubated by the female; incubation 24–29 days, young fledge at 21–29 days.

Food: Large insects, such as beetles and crickets; spiders, earthworms, small mammals, tree-frogs, small birds.

Miscellany: By providing special nestboxes, Scops Owls can be attracted to nest in villages.

1. Long-eared Owl; 2. Scops Owl; (Small picture on left) Young Long-eared Owl

1 Pygmy Owl

Glaucidium passerinum

(Owls)

The Pygmy Owl is the smallest European owl. Resident. Absent from Britain.

Identification: About the size of a Starling (17 cm). The small flat head and the yellow eyes are characteristic. Woodpecker-like flight.

Distribution: Northern and eastern Europe; in central Europe chiefly in mountainous regions.

Voice: Alarm call *'giu'*. Female call a high *'siiiie'*. Territorial song of male and female a piping *'piiu piiu piiu'*. In the autumn also a series of rapid climbing piping notes.

Habitat: Open coniferous forest with some deciduous trees, bogs and clearings; recently found also in lowland forest.

Breeding: Single-brooded (April to June). 3–7 white eggs, incubated by female; incubation 28–29 days, young fledge at 30–34 days.

Food: Mainly mice, also small birds, especially tits and finches.

Miscellany: In woods with Pygmy Owl territories, small birds utter feverish warning calls when the owls start singing. In Scandinavia the Pygmy Owl often hunts small birds at the bird table.

2 Little Owl

Athene noctua

(Owls)

The Little Owl is a typical bird of farmland. Resident. In Britain originally introduced.

Identification: Smaller than Feral Pigeon (22 cm), stocky and short-tailed, with flat head and large pale yellow eyes. Upperparts dark brown with dense white spotting.

Distribution: Europe except for Iceland, Ireland and northern Europe.

Voice: Call a piercing *'kviit'* or an upslurred *'uuhg'*. Territorial song of male a long drawn-out *'hu-ui'* or *'kivow'*.

Habitat: Open varied lowland farmland with small copses, meadows with pollarded willows, orchards by villages.

Breeding: Single-brooded (April to June). Nests in tree hole or hole in wall, also uses nestboxes. 3–5 white eggs, incubated by female; incubation 27–28 days, young fledge at 30–35 days.

Food: Chiefly mice, but also small birds, large insects, spiders, frogs, lizards and earthworms.

Miscellany: The Little Owl is often seen by day. The species can be helped by the provision of special nestboxes.

1. Pygmy Owl; 2. Little Owl; (Small picture on left) Young Little Owls

Kestrel

Falco tinnunculus

(Falcons)

The Kestrel is the commonest and most widespread small diurnal bird of prey in Europe; may be found almost anywhere in our countryside. Partial migrant. Resident in Britain.

Identification: Smaller than Carrion Crow (33–37 cm), rather long-tailed. Back of male brick-red, with broad black spots, crown, cheeks and tail grey, with black terminal band; no obvious cross-barring. Female upperparts cinnamon with strong dark spotting and cross-barring, underparts more strongly streaked than male, tail banded brown-black, with black terminal band.

Distribution: The whole of Europe except for Iceland and the far north of Scandinavia.

Voice: Calls frequently, especially during courtship and when breeding, a loud rapid 'kikikikiki...', a tremulous 'vriiii' or short 'tsick'.

Habitat: Open farmland with copses, woodland edge, villages; also in the centre of towns; common in parks with extensive open areas with short vegetation, suitable for hunting for rodents.

Breeding: Single-brooded (April to June). Breeds in the old nests of Crows and Magpies, rock ledges and holes in walls on tall buildings such as church towers. 4–6 yellowish eggs heavily spotted reddish-brown, incubated by the female; incubation 27–29 days, young fledge at 28–32 days.

Food: Chiefly field mice and voles, also shrews, small reptiles and young or weak birds.

Miscellany: Kestrels are often seen from the car as they sit on bushes or lamp standards beside the road on the lookout for mice; often seen hovering over meadows or fields. By providing nestboxes Kestrels can be encouraged to nest in towns. In winter they can be helped by scattering grain on a flat snow-free area; the Kestrels quickly learn to catch mice attracted to the grain!

1. The male is rather colourful; 2. The female (here with a recently caught vole) is barred and spotted; (Small picture on left) The 4–6 eggs are brooded by the female

1

2

1 Hobby

Falco subbuteo

(Falcons)

The Hobby is a swift and agile aerial hunter. Summer visitor; April to October.

Identification: Smaller than Carrion Crow (28–35 cm). Powerfully built small falcon with relatively short tail and long sickle-shaped wings; conspicuous dark moustache; rusty 'trousers' and vent. Young lack red below, upperparts with pale feather edges.

Distribution: Europe except for Iceland and much of northern and northwestern Europe. Winters in tropical Africa.

Voice: In spring a loud repeated 'gyiigyiigyiigyii...'.

Habitat: Open countryside such as heathland, marshes and lakesides, with copses and woodland edge; also in parkland and farmland.

Breeding: Single-brooded (June to August). Breeds in old crow and Magpie nests. 2–4 richly patterned red-brown eggs, incubated by the female. Incubation 28–31 days, young fledge at 28–34 days.

Food: Small birds caught in flight, dragonflies, beetles, grasshoppers.

Miscellany: Hobbies regularly hunt over wetlands for dragonflies and other large insects.

2 Sparrowhawk

Accipiter nisus

(Birds of prey)

The Sparrowhawk is an agile and daring hunter of small birds. Partial migrant on Continent. Resident in Britain.

Identification: Male thrush-sized (29 cm); female larger and distinctly heavier than the male (37 cm). Underparts finely barred, on a rusty background in male, and on whitish background in female.

Distribution: Europe except for Iceland and the far north of Scandinavia.

Voice: Call in spring in vicinity of nest a rapid and monotonous 'gigigigigi...'.

Habitat: Mixed and coniferous woodland with adjacent open countryside; parks and gardens.

Breeding: Single-brooded (May to July). Builds its own nest in trees, often in a conifer plantation. 4–6 pale grey eggs, splotched brown, incubated by the female; incubation 33–35 days, young fledge at 24–30 days.

Food: Almost entirely small birds.

Miscellany: The Sparrowhawk regularly hunts small birds in parks and gardens, especially in winter.

1. Hobby; 2. Female Sparrowhawk with prey, a House Sparrow; (Small picture on left) Hobby at nest

1

2

Pheasant

Phasianus colchicus

(Gamebirds)

The Pheasant is native to southern Asia and has been introduced with us for hunting. Resident.

Identification: About the size of a domestic chicken (male 66–89 cm; female 53–63 cm) with a long tail. Males colourful and very conspicuous. Females predominantly yellow-brown, marked black; shorter tail.

Distribution: Europe except for Iceland and large parts of northern and southern Europe.

Voice: In flight and when taking off often a hoarse crowing '*ekh-ekh*'. In spring the male's courtship call is a loud two-syllable squawking '*kuukuk*', followed by a loud clattering whirring of wings.

Habitat: Varied farmland with fields bordering open woodland and parks.

Breeding: Single-brooded (April to June). Well-hidden nest on the ground. 8–12 or more unmarked olive or brownish eggs, incubated by the female; incubation 23–24 days, young can fly at 12 days, but not fully grown and independent until after 2–3 months.

Food: Seeds, grain, plant matter, worms, snails, insects.

Miscellany: Pheasants are sociable in winter and often come to the edge of villages; they can be helped in icy weather by scattering grain.

Woodpigeon

Columba palumbus

(Pigeons and doves)

The Woodpigeon is common in parks in many towns. Partial migrant. Resident in Britain.

Identification: Larger than Feral Pigeon (41 cm). Large, long-tailed pigeon, with deep belly and conspicuous white markings on wings and neck in flight.

Distribution: Europe except for Iceland and parts of northern Scandinavia.

Voice: Territorial song is a muffled cooing '*ruguhgu gugu...*'.

Habitat: Open deciduous and mixed woodland, with surrounding meadows, fields, hedges and copses; parks and playing fields in towns and villages.

Breeding: Double-brooded (April to September). Platform twig nest, usually high in a tree, sometimes also on buildings. 2 white eggs, incubated by both sexes; incubation 16–17 days, young fledge at 28–31 days.

Food: Seeds, berries, fruits, grain, green plant material, clover, bread.

Miscellany: Woodpigeons take off and land with a characteristic clattering wing noise.

1. Pair of Pheasants, male on left, female on right; 2. Woodpigeon on the nest; 3. Woodpigeons; (Small picture on left) Nest and eggs of Woodpigeon

Stock Dove
Columba oenas

(Pigeons and doves)

The Stock Dove is our only pigeon which nests in old woodpecker holes.
Resident. Summer visitor to central and eastern Europe.

Identification: About the size of Feral Pigeon (33 cm), but rather slimmer
and always with a grey rump; lacks white markings on the wings and neck.

Distribution: Europe except for Iceland and much of northern Europe and
the Alps.

Voice: Territorial song of male a muffled, rapidly repeated *'oh-ruo oh-ruo...'*.

Habitat: Deciduous and mixed woodland with old trees and large holes;
also in suitable parkland. Feeds in fields.

Breeding: 2–3 broods a year (April to September). Builds a nest of twigs,
stems and leaves in an old woodpecker-hole or nestbox. 2 white eggs,
incubated by both sexes; incubation 16–18 days, young fledge at 23–28 days.

Food: Seeds, fruits, green plant material, berries, clover.

Miscellany: Stock Doves are strongly dependent on finding holes to nest in
and often quickly occupy suitable nestboxes. Outside the nesting season
Stock Doves flock with other pigeons to feed in harvested fields.

Feral Pigeon
Columba livia f. domestica

(Pigeons and doves)

In many parks and gardens Feral or Town Pigeons, derived from escaped
domestic doves and racing pigeons, are amongst the commonest birds.
Resident.

Identification: (33 cm). Plumage very variable, reflecting the many varieties
of Domestic Pigeon, though most are predominantly dove-grey, with two
black bars on wing, and white rump and lower back.

Distribution: Human settlements throughout the whole of Europe.

Voice: The characteristic muffled cooing *'guhgu-guruh'* may be heard
throughout the year.

Habitat: Mainly towns and cities – numerous in squares, parks, zoos and
open spaces.

Breeding: 3–4 broods a year (mostly March to September). Nest of twigs,
roots and stems, often under bridges, in holes in walls, on ledges on
buildings and balconies. 2 white eggs, incubated by both sexes; incubation
17–18 days, young fledge from about 25 days.

Food: Seeds, grain, buds, shoots,
leaves, bread, scraps.

Miscellany: The feeding of Feral
Pigeons has become a problem in
many places, as these 'flying rats'
multiply rapidly as a result, and
destroy old buildings with their
droppings.

1. Stock Dove; 2. Feral Pigeon;
(Small picture on left) Stock Dove
at nest hole in tree

1   Collared Dove

Streptopelia decaocto

(Pigeons and doves)

The Collared Dove arrived with us only about 40 years ago from the southeast, and is now common everywhere around settlements. Resident.

Identification: Smaller than Feral Pigeon (32 cm), and distinctly slimmer and longer-tailed. Beige plumage with pinkish flush on breast and conspicuous black neck collar.

Distribution: Europe, except for Iceland and most of Scandinavia and the Iberian peninsula.

Voice: Calls frequently in flight a nasal *'hhvii hhvii'*. Territorial song of the male a monotonous cooing *'gu-guh-gu gu-guh-gu'*.

Habitat: Settlements of all types, including farms; common in gardens, zoos and parks where fed.

Breeding: 2–4 broods a year (March to October). Platform nest of dry twigs and roots, usually in a fork in a tree or bush, but also on and in buildings. 2 white eggs, incubated by both sexes; incubation 14–18 days, young fledge at 16–19 days.

Food: Seeds, green plant matter, buds, grain, fruits, bread.

Miscellany: Collared Doves perform display flights early in the spring, gliding down on depressed wings, calling loudly.

2/3   Turtle Dove

Streptopelia turtur

(Pigeons and doves)

The Turtle Dove is the smallest European pigeon. Summer visitor; April to October.

Identification: Much smaller and slimmer than Feral Pigeon (26–28 cm). Upperparts patterned rufous and black, with conspicuous black-and-white striped patch on side of neck.

Distribution: Europe except for Iceland, Ireland, Scotland and Scandinavia; only in warm, dry regions, so with a rather patchy distribution.

Voice: Territorial song of the male a monotonous purring *'turrr-turrr-turrr-turrr...'*.

Habitat: Woodland edge, meadows, copses, orchards; also in parks and large gardens with deciduous trees.

Breeding: Double-brooded (May to August). Platform twig nest in bushes or trees. 2 white eggs, incubated by both sexes; incubation 13–16 days, young fledge at 18–23 days.

Food: Seeds of weeds and grasses, conifer seeds.

Miscellany: Flight appears dashing and somewhat jerky.

1. Collared Dove; 2. Turtle Dove; 3. Turtle Dove with young in nest; (Small picture on left) Turtle Dove nest and eggs

1

2

3

Great Crested Grebe

Podiceps cristatus

(Grebes)

The Great Crested Grebe is our largest grebe. Partial migrant.

Identification: About the size of Mallard (46–50 cm), but much slimmer and longer-necked. Unmistakable in spring with its striking chestnut and black head-dress. Outside the breeding season loses head and neck adornments, plain-coloured. Young striped on head and neck.

Distribution: Europe except for Iceland and most of Scandinavia.

Voice: A hoarse loud '*gruck gruck*' or deep '*orrr*'.

Habitat: Large ponds and lakes, reservoirs.

Breeding: 1–2 broods (April to July). Floating nest of reeds and waterweed, usually well hidden among reeds or rushes. 3–5 eggs, at first whitish, becoming stained brownish, incubated by both sexes; incubation 27–29 days, young independent after 10–11 weeks of care from both parents.

Food: Fish, crustaceans, aquatic insects.

Miscellany: Great Crested Grebes perform striking courtship displays in spring with synchronised head shaking, neck-stretching and surfacing with weed.

Little Grebe

Tachybaptus ruficollis

(Grebes)

The Little Grebe is our smallest European grebe. Partial migrant.

Identification: Only a little bigger than Blackbird (25–28 cm), dumpy and short-necked. In breeding plumage head and neck chestnut-brown. In winter plumage a sober yellowish-brown.

Distribution: Europe except for Iceland and most of Scandinavia.

Voice: In spring a long attention-grabbing trill, uttered by male and female in duet.

Habitat: Small thickly-vegetated lakes and ponds; also on suitable park lakes. In winter in small flocks on lakes and rivers, including in towns.

Breeding: Double-brooded (April to July). Floating nest of rotting vegetation concealed among vegetation under the bank. 4–6 whitish eggs, incubated by both sexes; incubation 20–21 days, young independent at about 5 to 6 weeks.

Food: Insects, snails, tadpoles, small crustaceans and fish.

Miscellany: In winter Little Grebes are recognised by their thickly fluffed-up rear-end.

1. Pair of Great Crested Grebes with young; 2. Great Crested Grebe in winter; 3. Little Grebe in winter; 4. Little Grebe with two young; (Small picture on left) Great Crested Grebe at nest

1 Grey Heron

Ardea cinerea

(Herons)

The Grey Heron is the commonest species of heron in Europe, and indeed in many regions the only heron. Partial migrant. Resident in Britain.

Identification: Smaller than White Stork (90–96 cm). Plumage predominantly grey; head and neck mainly white, with two long black plumes from back of head.

Distribution: Europe except for Iceland and most of northern Europe; in most of southern Europe only in winter.

Voice: Call in flight a loud hoarse croaking 'kreik'.

Habitat: Waterside with shallow banks for fishing, wet meadows for rodent-catching.

Breeding: Single-brooded (March to June). Colonial nester; huge stick nest usually high in trees. 3–5 pale blue-green eggs, incubated by both sexes; incubation 25–28 days, young fledge at 50–55 days.

Food: Fish, small mammals, such as voles and moles, frogs, reptiles and large insects.

Miscellany: The Grey Heron often stands motionless at the edge of reeds on the lookout for prey. In flight neck held retracted in 'S'.

2 White Stork

Ciconia ciconia

(Storks)

The White Stork is well known in folklore as the bringer of new-born babies. Summer visitor; end of March to early September. Rare visitor to Britain.

Identification: Large wading bird (100–115 cm). Bill and legs red; plumage mostly white with black flight feathers. Young birds with brownish legs and bill.

Distribution: Central, eastern and southeast Europe, the Iberian peninsula, North Africa. Winters in southern Africa.

Voice: Bill-clappering greeting when nesting.

Habitat: Open varied farmland, not too intensively cultivated, with wet meadows and waterbodies.

Breeding: Single-brooded (April to June). Large nest on house roofs, chimneys, pylons and trees. 3–5 white eggs, incubated by both sexes; incubation 32–34 days, young fledge at 58–64 days.

Food: Mice, earthworms, insects, frogs, snakes.

Miscellany: In flight the White Stork is easily identified by its black-and-white wing-pattern and long outstretched neck.

1. Grey Heron; 2. Adult White Stork with 4 young; (Small picture on left) Small young White Storks in nest

Mute Swan

Cygnus olor

(Wildfowl)

The Mute Swan is our heaviest waterbird. Resident. In central Europe it was originally introduced as an ornamental bird, but has greatly increased and colonised all suitable waters.

Identification: Larger than domestic goose (145–160 cm). Pure white; orange-red bill with black basal knob, which is biggest in the spring male. Young mostly grey-brown with lead-grey bill, lacking basal knob. Some young are white even in their first plumage.

Distribution: British Isles, southern Scandinavia, central and eastern Europe.

Voice: Not very vocal, sometimes a snoring *'ga-yarr'* or a loud hissing.

Habitat: Lowland lakes and rivers; characteristic resident of many park lakes, even in the middle of cities.

Breeding: Single-brooded (April to June). Large nest pile of reed and waterside vegetation, mostly close to the water's edge. 5–7 eggs, at first greyish-green, later becoming stained brownish, brooded by female; incubation 35–40 days, young fledge at 4–5 months.

Food: Chiefly submerged plants, which are torn from the bottom making use of their long neck, also various waterside plants. Park swans come in large numbers to stale bread; this can lead to serious water pollution.

Miscellany: Even from afar the Mute Swan can be recognised by the carriage of its neck in a gentle S-shape. In flight the wings make a distinctive whistling noise, unlike the other two swan species. In winter swans often gather into large flocks and visit park lakes, jetties or other spots where waterbirds are fed. The close proximity of other swans leads in spring to bitter fights for territory, as each pair requires quite a large area of water, which they defend vigorously against intruding pairs.

1. The young are literally ferried by their mother; 2. Both partners take a share of nest building, the male gathering most of the material; (Small picture on left) Adult with eggs and newly-hatched young

Whooper Swan

Cygnus cygnus

(Wildfowl)

The Whooper Swan attains the same length as the Mute Swan, but not the same weight. Winter visitor, from October to April.

Identification: Larger than domestic goose (145–160 cm). Like Mute Swan, but bill black with extensive yellow base, no bill-knob and with head and neck held more erect.

Distribution: Iceland and northern Europe. In the rest of Europe only as a winter visitor.

Voice: Call in flight a loud trumpeting, usually di- or trisyllabic, 'huup-huup-(huup)'; also when swimming nasal, goose-like notes.

Habitat: Breeds mainly on boggy lakes of the northern taiga and tundra zones; in winter on coasts and large lakes, including park lakes in the north.

Breeding: Single-brooded (May to July). Large nest of water plants, usually on a small island. 3–7 creamy eggs, incubated by the female; incubation 33–40 days, young fledge at around 3 months.

Food: Submerged vegetation; on land, grass and cereals.

Miscellany: Whooper Swans are commonly found on land, grazing like geese on grass and young cereals.

Canada Goose

Branta canadensis

(Wildfowl)

The Canada Goose is an introduction with us from its North American homeland. Resident.

Identification: Larger than Greylag Goose (90–110 cm). Conspicuous black-and-white head pattern; bill, neck, legs and tail all black.

Distribution: In Europe found in the British Isles, Scandinavia, and a number of sites in central Europe.

Voice: Flight-call a loud nasal trumpeting – recalling Whooper Swan rather than other geese.

Habitat: Lakes, fish-ponds, gravel pits and other small waterbodies; semi-tame birds common on park lakes, even in the middle of cities.

Breeding: Single-brooded (March to June). Large nest of plant material, often on a small island. 5–6 creamy eggs, incubated by the female; incubation 28–30 days, young fledge at 40–48 days.

Food: A variety of grasses and weeds, roots, seeds, water-plants. On park lakes Canada Geese often come for bread.

Miscellany: Outside the nesting season, family parties gather into large flocks. Not infrequently pairs with Greylag Goose producing young showing features of both parents.

1. Whooper Swans; 2. Pair of Canada Geese with young

Greylag Goose

Anser anser

(Wildfowl)

The Greylag Goose has become well-known as the main species studied by the behavioural scientist Konrad Lorenz. Partial migrant.

Identification: The size of domestic goose (75–90 cm), of which it is the ancestor. Plumage uniformly grey-brown, flesh-pink legs; bill pinkish (eastern race), or orange-yellow (western race).

Distribution: Iceland, Scandinavia, British Isles, central and eastern Europe. Birds in lowland Britain the result of introductions.

Voice: The calls correspond essentially to the loud clear calls of the farmyard goose '*aahng-aahng*'; contact call '*gagaga*'.

Habitat: Large lakes with fringing vegetation, bogs, marshy woods. Feeds in meadows and pasture. A common bird of park lakes and gravel pits, often in large flocks.

Breeding: Single-brooded (April to July). Large nest in inaccessible site near water. 4–8 whitish eggs, incubated by the female; incubation 27–29 days, young fledge at about 8 weeks.

Food: Various grasses, weeds, very fond of clover, dandelions.

Miscellany: Flying Greylags can be identified at long range by their pale silvery-grey upperwing coverts and the clear call.

Bar-headed Goose

Anser indicus

(Wildfowl)

The Bar-headed Goose comes originally from the high plateaus of the Himalayas and was introduced into Europe as an ornamental bird.

Identification: Smaller than domestic goose (70–82 cm). The pale overall impression and the characteristic barred head pattern are unmistakable.

Distribution: Occasional escape in Britain. Common ornamental park bird in Germany. Free-living birds there originate from introduction attempts or escapes from captivity.

Voice: Not so far-carrying and tuneful as Greylag and Canada Goose.

Habitat: Usually park lakes.

Breeding: Single-brooded (May to June). Platform nest in boggy areas. 4–6 eggs. Incubation 27–30 days, young fledge at 7–8 weeks.

Food: Grass, weed roots, grain, bread.

Miscellany: Bar-headed Geese often associate with Greylag Geese; sometimes mixed pairs of the two species are formed.

1. Greylag Goose; 2. Greylag Goose with young; 3. Bar-headed Goose; (Small picture on left) Nest and eggs of Greylag Goose

Mallard

Anas platyrhynchos

(Wildfowl)

The Mallard is the ancestor of most domestic ducks; it is not only our largest dabbling duck, but also by far the commonest European duck. Partial migrant.

Identification: Large stocky duck (55–60 cm). Male in winter with bottle-green head, yellow bill, pale grey upperparts, with black stern and curly tail feathers; in eclipse plumage similar to female, but lacking black on bill and altogether rather darker. Female predominantly brown, bill orange with more or less extensive black markings at base and on top.

Distribution: The whole of Europe except for high mountain regions.

Voice: Female a loud quacking, falling in pitch *'waaak-wak-wak-wak-wak-wak'*. Call of male a muffled hoarse *'riib riib'* and a high whistling *'piu'*.

Habitat: All types of waters: from small pools through large lakes to slowly flowing rivers with rich fringing vegetation. Common on park lakes and garden ponds.

Breeding: Single-brooded (March to June). Neatly constructed nest of stems from the surrounding vegetation, lined with down, usually very well hidden and close to water; in reeds, under bushes, in willow pollards, but also on buildings or in nesting baskets. 7–12 greenish or yellowish eggs, incubated by the female; incubation 26–29 days, young fledge at 50–60 days.

Food: Seeds of aquatic and land plants, green plant material, insects, worms, snails, crustaceans, bread, kitchen scraps.

Miscellany: The Mallard is also sometimes known simply as the 'Wild Duck'. It is often the most numerous bird on park lakes where the birds are fed. From autumn to spring communal displays take place in which the drakes are the participants and the ducks merely spectators; a variety of behaviours can be studied, including 'Head-flicks', 'Upward-shakes' and 'Nod-swimming'.

1. The pair remain together in spring until the female starts laying; 2. The incubating female is difficult to make out in her brown camouflage plumage; 3. The young brood take a rest on land in a meadow; (Small picture on left) The clutch contains up to 10 eggs

Gadwall

Anas strepera

(Wildfowl)

Both sexes of Gadwall are rather unobtrusive and the species is therefore easily overlooked. Partial migrant.

Identification: A little smaller and slimmer than Mallard (48–52 cm). Males in winter predominantly brown and grey with black stern. Females and eclipse males very similar to female Mallard, but with white speculum and orange band along edge of bill.

Distribution: Eastern Europe; in rest of Europe patchily distributed, north to Iceland, Scotland and southern Sweden.

Voice: Female call similar to that of female Mallard, but a little higher and more penetrating; during courtship male utters a deep *'erp'* and *'tuh tuh'*.

Habitat: Only in lowlands; shallow lakes and slowly flowing, large rivers with luxuriant bankside vegetation; in some districts also on park lakes.

Breeding: Single-brooded (May to July). 8–12 creamy-buff eggs, incubated by the female; incubation 25–27 days, young fledge at about 7 weeks.

Food: Various aquatic plants and seeds; only very occasionally small animals.

Miscellany: Gadwalls are easily identified in flight by their white speculum.

Mandarin

Aix galericulata

(Wildfowl)

The drake Mandarin is our most colourful duck and correspondingly sought after as an ornamental bird. Resident.

Identification: Smaller than Mallard (42–48 cm). Male very colourful and quite unmistakable; especially striking are the erect orange 'sails' in the wing. Female rather soberly coloured with white eye-ring extending back towards nape.

Distribution: Originally from eastern Asia; introduced in various places in Europe, ornamental birds often seen on park lakes, but also now quite naturalised locally and self-sustaining.

Voice: In flight male utters a piping *'vrrick'*; the female's call is a Coot-like *'kett'*.

Habitat: Wooded lakes and rivers with thick bankside vegetation; sometimes comes to be fed on park lakes.

Breeding: Single-brooded (April to June). Nests in tree hole close to water, occasionally also on the ground in thick undergrowth. 9–12 white eggs, incubated by the female; incubation 28–30 days, young independent after 40–45 days.

Food: Vegetable matter, seeds, nuts, acorns, grain, worms, snails, insects.

Miscellany: As Mandarins often choose a hole high in a tree for nesting, the young have to jump to the ground after hatching; they normally survive the fall unscathed.

1. Male Gadwall; 2. Female Gadwall; 3. Mandarin pair, female on left, male on right

1

2

3

Pochard

Aythya ferina

(Wildfowl)

The Pochard is a common winter visitor, and a familiar sight on many park lakes. Partial migrant.

Identification: Smaller than Mallard (43–47 cm), stocky build, long high head with shallow sloping forehead. With its chestnut-brown head, red eye, black breast and silver grey body, the male is hard to confuse with other ducks. Female rather plain brown with paler head markings.

Distribution: Europe except for the greater part of Scandinavia. In the Iberian peninsula and southern Europe almost entirely a winter visitor.

Voice: Call of female a hoarse croaking *'kharr kharr'*; in courtship the male utters a soft whistling *'uiviyerr'*.

Habitat: Shallow reed-fringed lakes, fishponds; outside the breeding season on waterbodies of all types, including large park lakes, even in the middle of cities.

Breeding: Single-brooded (May to July). Nest well hidden in bankside vegetation. 8–11 greyish-green eggs, incubated by the female; incubation 24–27 days, young fledge at around 7–8 weeks.

Food: Aquatic plants, seeds, insect larvae, worms, snails, grain.

Miscellany: Flying Pochards make a characteristic whistling noise with their wings.

Tufted Duck

Aythya fuligula

(Wildfowl)

The Tufted Duck is usually our second-commonest duck in winter, after the Mallard. Partial migrant.

Identification: Smaller than Mallard (41–45 cm). Male strikingly black-and-white, with long drooping head tuft and yellow eye. Female plain dark brown, with only a suggestion of a tuft.

Distribution: Northern Europe and Iceland; British Isles, northern France, central and eastern Europe.

Voice: In courtship male utters a chick-like tremulous whistle; call of female a hard rasping *'err-err-err'*.

Habitat: Large lakes and reservoirs; in winter in large numbers on still and flowing waters, also on park lakes in the middle of cities.

Breeding: Single-brooded (May to August). Well-hidden nest in bankside vegetation or in reeds. 8–11 pale greyish-green eggs, incubated by the female; incubation 23–26 days, young fledge at about 7 weeks.

Food: Mussels, snails, crustaceans, insect larvae, seeds of aquatic plants.

Miscellany: On many park lakes or at jetties Tufted Ducks join with Mallards, Coots and Black-headed Gulls to be fed with bread.

1. Pair of Pochards, female on left, male on right; 2. Pair of Tufted Ducks, female on right, male on left; 3. Tufted Duck with young

Goldeneye

Bucephala clangula

(Wildfowl)

The Goldeneye is a northern diving duck, in Britain breeding only in Scotland, though increasing. Mainly a winter visitor.

Identification: Smaller than Mallard (43–48 cm). Stocky diving duck with strikingly large triangular head and yellow eye. Male black-and-white with a roundish white patch in front of the eye. Female and young male with mainly grey plumage and brown head.

Distribution: Scotland, northern Europe, occasional further south in central and eastern Europe.

Voice: Call of female in flight a rasping '*karrr karrr*'. Male in display a squawking '*kvi-riik*'.

Habitat: Lakes in wooded countryside and slow flowing rivers; outside the breeding season on larger waterbodies of all sorts, including park lakes.

Breeding: Single-brooded (May to July). Uses old Black Woodpecker holes or special nestboxes. 6–11 blue-green eggs, incubated by the female; incubation 27–32 days. Young jump from the nest-hole after hatching.

Food: Small crustaceans, mussels, snails, fish, insects, seeds.

Miscellany: Goldeneyes are fast fliers on rapidly beating wings; even from a distance their distinctive whistling wing noise can be heard.

Goosander

Mergus merganser

(Wildfowl)

Goosanders are large ducks with long narrow bills, hooked at the tip. Partial migrant and winter visitor.

Identification: Larger than Mallard (60–66 cm). Male largely white, head black with dark green gloss, back black; female mainly grey with sharply demarcated brown head; in winter both sexes show a delicate pink flush on the underparts.

Distribution: Northern Europe, including Iceland; northern and western Britain, scattered in central Europe.

Voice: In courtship male utters a high '*kriu-ro*'.

Habitat: Clear lakes and rivers, especially in wooded countryside. Outside the breeding season on lakes, reservoirs, rivers. Locally, also on park lakes.

Breeding: Single-brooded (April to June). Nests in large tree hole or in special nestbox. 8–12 cream-coloured eggs, incubated by the female; incubation 30–33 days, young fledge at 8–9 weeks.

Food: Fish, crustaceans.

Miscellany: Often seen swimming with head and neck submerged, on the lookout for fish.

1. Pair of Goldeneyes, female on left, male on right; 2. Goosander with young; 3. Male Goosanders, with female on right; (Small picture on left) Nest and eggs of Goldeneye

Moorhen

Gallinula chloropus

(Crakes and rails)

The Moorhen is a small chicken-like waterbird, commonly met with on park lakes. Resident.

Identification: Smaller than Coot (32–35 cm), with long toes. Sooty plumage and red bill with yellow tip, red frontal shield, conspicuous white undertail coverts. Young brownish, chicks with colourful head pattern.

Distribution: Europe except for Iceland and the greater part of Scandinavia.

Voice: Call a sharp rolling *'kiurrk'* or *'kirreck'*.

Habitat: Lakes, ponds and slow-flowing rivers with luxuriant waterside vegetation; frequently on suitable streams and ponds in villages and parks, even in cities.

Breeding: 1–3 broods a year (April to August). Bowl-shaped nest well concealed in waterside vegetation. 5–10 cream-coloured eggs with speckled pattern, incubated by the female; incubation 19–22 days, young fledge at 40–50 days.

Food: Wetland and aquatic plants, seeds, fruits, insects, worms, snails.

Miscellany: Moorhens swim with rhythmical head movements and frantic tail-twitching showing off their snow-white undertail coverts.

Coot

Fulica atra

(Crakes and rails)

The Coot is one of the commonest waterbirds in our parks. Partial migrant.

Identification: A dumpy rail (36–38 cm); plumage uniform black, with white bill and frontal shield; toes lobed.

Distribution: Europe except for Iceland and the greater part of Scandinavia.

Voice: Call a loud barking *'kiv'* or *'kuck'* and a hard *'pix'*.

Habitat: Lakes, ponds and reservoirs, rivers; common on park lakes, also in villages and towns.

Breeding: 1–2 broods (April to July). Large nest of aquatic vegetation, often well hidden, usually in shallow water. 5–10 whitish eggs, finely speckled, incubated by both sexes; incubation 21–24 days, young independent at about 8 weeks.

Food: Aquatic plants, reed shoots, grass, invertebrates, bread. Also seeks food on land.

Miscellany: Coots take off from the water by running along the surface, beating the water with their wings and pattering with their feet.

1. Moorhen; 2. Immature Moorhens; 3. Coot with 3 young; (Small picture on left) Moorhen nest with eggs and newly-hatched young

1

2

3

Black-headed Gull

Larus ridibundus

(Gulls)

Inland the Black-headed Gull is generally the commonest gull. Partial migrant and winter visitor.

Identification: Size of Feral Pigeon (38–41 cm). In spring with chocolate brown head and dark red bill; outside breeding season head is white with dark mark on ear coverts, bill pale reddish.

Distribution: Europe except for parts of Scandinavia; chiefly a winter visitor to the Iberian peninsula and southern Europe.

Voice: Call a frequently uttered loud screeching 'kveer', 'krrriya', 'gegegeg'.

Habitat: Nests in colonies on lake shores and small islands in lakes. In winter on rubbish tips, at sewage works, piers and jetties and on park lakes.

Breeding: Single-brooded (April to July). Nest of stalks and stems. 3 brown to olive eggs variably blotched darker, incubated by both sexes; incubation 23–24 days, young fledge at 5–6 weeks.

Food: Aquatic insects, fish, worms, crustaceans, carrion, scraps, bread.

Miscellany: Black-headed Gulls, with their loud screeching and quarrelling, are a familiar part of the winter scene in many towns, where they besiege bridges or park lakes. The larger Herring and Lesser Black-headed Gulls frequent rubbish tips and playing fields in winter.

Common Gull

Larus canus

(Gulls)

The Common Gull is a common inland visitor outside the breeding season. Partial migrant and winter visitor.

Identification: A little bigger than Black-headed Gull (40–43 cm). A slender gull with white roundish head, slim greenish-yellow bill and dark eyes. In winter head and neck finely streaked brownish-grey.

Distribution: Northern Europe including Iceland; British Isles. In central Europe mainly coastal, though also common on inland lakes in winter.

Voice: Call a drawn-out 'klii-ya' or 'ka-ka-ka', when alarmed 'pee-yiih'.

Habitat: Sea coasts, marshy meadows, lake shores; in winter often on jetties or park lakes.

Breeding: Single-brooded (May to July). 3 olive or brownish eggs variably speckled, incubated by both sexes; incubation 23–28 days, young fledge at 5 weeks.

Food: Fish, fish scraps, worms, mussels, insects, mice, bread, scraps.

Miscellany: Where waterbirds are fed, Common Gulls are usually more retiring than the pushy Black-headed Gulls.

1. Black-headed Gull in spring; 2. Black-headed Gull in non-breeding dress; 3. Common Gull; (Small picture on left) Nest and eggs of Black-headed Gull

1

2

3

Helping birds in the garden

The Red List of threatened or declining animal species is becoming steadily longer. The destruction of formerly unspoilt countryside is increasing dramatically through the rapid spread of settlements and roads. Intensive agriculture and forestry leave scanty habitat for wild birds. Therefore parks and gardens, which are not primarily used for cultivation, have become increasingly important as a substitute habitat for our birds.

If you want to help birds in an effective way, you can create a suitable habitat with a natural wild garden. At the end of this book you will find an illustration of a bird-friendly garden. The various items of bird equipment in the drawing are labelled with numbers and are explained below:

The establishment of a hedge of native bushes and shrubs offers protection from enemies of all sorts; moreover insect-eating birds such as Blackcap and Garden Warbler, Chiffchaff and Willow Warbler, find natural nest sites there. By planting native berry-bearing shrubs and transforming a well-mown lawn into a colourful wildflower meadow, you will create a diversity of nature in the garden and thus suitable food sources for many birds. A small wilderness area with tall grass, raspberry canes and brambles offers warblers, Yellowhammers and Dunnocks cover. A pile of brushwood (12) comprising twigs of a variety of thicknesses will be readily adopted as a nesting site by Wrens and Robins. In part of the garden at least, leaves should be left to lie where they have fallen in autumn from trees and shrubs. They protect the ground in winter from drying out and provide food for insects and earthworms, the preferred food of Blackbirds, Song Thrushes and Starlings. Also a compost heap will be readily investigated by these birds for insects and vegetable scraps.

A bird-bath (8) should be a feature of every bird-friendly garden: an old plate or a hollow in the ground lined with foil is sufficient to attract thirsty and bathing birds. Be sure to take care that around the bird bath the vegetation is kept low so that cats and other enemies cannot creep up unseen. The bath can also be placed on a post – then hunting cats do not have a chance and the bird gardener can more easily watch the birds at a comfortable height.

Also, an overgrown house wall is suitable as a substitute habitat for birds. Climbing plants such as ivy, vines, honeysuckle and Clematis offer Blackbirds, Song Thrushes, Robins, Spotted Flycatchers and many other bird species good nesting sites. These plants also protect the house wall from rain, retain the heat and absorb the dust.

Providing nesting opportunities in the garden and on the house

As natural nest sites for hole-nesting birds are often in short supply in built-up areas, the 'housing shortage' can be relieved by the provision of nestboxes. Even though these artificial holes cannot replace the variety of natural sites such as woodpecker-holes, rot-holes in branches or bark crevices, they nevertheless offer the chance to attract many birds to breed close to man. Nestboxes can either be home-made from wood or they may be bought, for example in a garden centre. There is a wide choice of wood and wood/concrete boxes – also unfortunately in plastic which is totally unsuitable, as it overheats in summer. Care must be taken when putting up the boxes: cats and weasels must be unable to gain entry (6). The entrance hole should face east, away from the direction of most bad weather, and the box should be sheltered from full sun and rain. The size of the hole is crucial for the occupation of the box: small tits (Coal and Blue Tits) require 26–28 mm (4); Great Tit, Nuthatch, Pied Flycatcher 32 mm; an elongated oval for Redstart should be 45 mm high and 30 mm wide; the Starling nests for preference in a box with a 50 mm hole (1). The internal dimensions of ' the base for the smaller hole-nesters should be at least 15 x 15 cm (12 cm diameter in round boxes), for larger species correspondingly greater. Special Little Owl nestboxes (3) are 80–100 cm long, with a diameter of 17–19 cm. Ideally you should find out from specialist suppliers about appropriate protection measures against weasels and other bird enemies, as the success of the nestbox depends above all on such protection. In autumn, after the young have flown, the old nest must be removed, as otherwise parasites such as bird fleas can multiply. For this reason, as a rule small birds build a new nest for each brood. In addition, you should clean the nestbox thoroughly (but not with poisonous substances), and then put it back up immediately, as in winter it serves the birds as a sheltered roosting site.

For Redstarts, Spotted Flycatchers and Pied Wagtails, which can be called 'open hole nesters', open-fronted boxes (9) can be placed in protected sites in trees or on house walls. These boxes are open at the front and are a substitute for rot-holes or rock ledges and crevices. Treecreeper boxes (2) have a side entrance. Artificial swallow nests are placed outside under the eaves for House Martins (10), and inside on rafters for Swallows (11). In addition a muddy puddle can be made to provide nest-building material for these birds (7).

Free-nesting birds can also be helped by providing piles of brushwood in which Wrens, Robins and other species can build their nests. A 'nest whirl' (5) can be made by simply tying together several twigs, to provide a circular nest foundation for various bush- and tree-nesters.

How to help lost baby birds

In late spring and summer when our garden birds are rearing their young, you will sometimes come across a seemingly abandoned young bird. With its short tail, the remnants of down on its head and back, and its persistent begging call, it seems so pitiful and helpless that you are tempted to take it home and feed it. You must not be too hasty, and must first ascertain that the fledgling really is orphaned. In fact, the young of many birds leave the nest before they can fly. They wait in safe cover for their parents to bring them food, and let them know where they are with their characteristic begging call. You should therefore watch the young bird for some time. If it is in the open put it carefully into the cover of a tree or bush. Then watch from a distance to see if the fledgling is being fed. If the parents do not appear after a couple of hours, and if the fledgling is sitting around listlessly, it really is lost and needs your help. Such a case is the exception, as the majority of young birds you will find are not lost, but unfortunately cannot yet fly very well. The rearing of a baby bird is often difficult and is a job for the expert; fledglings have a much better chance of survival in the wild! Moreover, by taking songbirds home, you risk breaking the bird protection laws.

Contrary to popular opinion, a young bird, even if it has been handled, will not be abandoned by its parents for this reason. Only mammals with a strongly developed sense of smell such as roe-deer and hares abandon their young when they have been touched by a human hand! Every year tens of thousands of baby birds are handled and ringed by bird ringers for research purposes – without them being left by their parents to go hungry.

A genuinely orphaned young bird should ideally be placed in a flower pot lined with warm material (flannel, hay) and placed in a quiet dark place. Between feeds a woollen cover is placed carefully over the bird, so that it does not get cold. Every 1–2 hours the fledgling is given, with a blunt pair of tweezers, a pellet of low-fat curd cheese, soft food containing many insects, hard-boiled egg and finely chopped raw heart. The young bird should also be given a little water, especially in hot weather. After this initial help, the young bird should be taken as soon as possible to an expert in a bird hospital, as the rearing of a young bird demands great expertise. So that it can be fed the correct type of food, its identity must first be established and that can be very difficult with many baby birds. Therefore remember, for the bird's sake: young birds should not be taken home, but left in the wild.

How do I identify an unknown bird?

The bird enthusiast does not need to travel to a distant bird paradise to study the life and behaviour of his or her feathered friends. For the large number of birds around the house and in the garden offer a wealth of possibilities for interesting observations. You can learn to identify the commonest garden birds, such as Blackbird, Greenfinch, Great and Blue Tits, Robin and Starling, quickly and with certainty. Therefore a few observations on this subject and identification tips follow.

It is not always easy to determine to which species a bird belongs, or to which sex – if male and female appear different. As a rule you only see the bird for a short time and must, before it flies off, note as many details as possible about its appearance and behaviour. In this way familiarity with our commonest birds helps. For example, a Dunnock can be identified as such by simply comparing it with the universally known House Sparrow (*the* Sparrow), and noting that it has a much slimmer bill and quite different behaviour. It is also sensible to take the time to become familiar with the appearance, behaviour and lifestyle of common bird species, before trying to identify unknown birds. If you know these 'reference species' well, the first step has already been taken on the long road to becoming a 'bird expert'.

For bird identification particularly important features are size and shape; the estimation of size is nevertheless often difficult for we are influenced by distance and light conditions. Further identification features to be looked for are the appearance of bill and tail (both length and shape), leg-length, as well as striking plumage features (colours and contrasts, noticeable eyestripes and wing- or tail-bars). In flight both wing-length and -shape should be noted. Of great significance are voice as well as conspicuous behavioural clues such as how the bird moves on the ground (whether hopping, running, walking) or the way it flies. The advanced birder also takes into consideration in his identification habitat and time of year of the occurrence, and is able therefore to exclude one or another species from consideration: a Skylark in thick conifer forest is very unlikely, similarly a Willow Warbler in January.

According to the species one or another of the chosen criteria for identification may be decisive, but often only the simultaneous consideration of several features leads to the answer. Practice and experience are of course the most important requirements for successful species identification.

INDEX

Accipiter nisus, 122
Acrocephalus scirpaceus, 34
Aegithalos caudatus, 56
Aix galericulata, 142
Alauda arvensis, 6
Alcedo atthis, 100
Anas platyrhynchos, 140
Anas strepera, 142
Anser anser, 138
Anser indicus, 138
Apus apus, 100
Ardea cinerea, 132
Asio otus, 116
Athene noctua, 118
Aythya ferina, 144
Aythya fuligula, 144
Bar-headed Goose, 138
Barn Owl, 112
Black Redstart, 22
Black-headed Gull, 150
Blackbird, 26
Blackcap, 38
Blue Tit, 52
Bombycilla garrulus, 14
Brambling, 82
Branta canadensis, 136
Bucephala clangula, 146
Bullfinch, 90
Bunting, Cirl, 98
Bunting, Ortolan, 98
Canada Goose, 136
Carduelis cannabina, 92
Carduelis carduelis, 88
Carduelis chloris, 86
Carduelis flammea, 88
Carduelis spinus, 84
Carpodacus erythrinus, 92
Carrion Crow, 74
Certhia brachydactyla, 60
Certhia familiaris, 60
Chaffinch, 80
Chiffchaff, 42
Ciconia ciconia, 132
Cinclus cinclus, 16
Cirl Bunting, 98
Coal Tit, 56
Coccothraustes coccothraustes, 82
Collared Dove, 128
Collared Flycatcher, 46
Columba livia f. domestica, 126
Columba oenas, 126
Columba palumbus, 124
Common Gull, 150

Common Rosefinch, 92
Common Whitethroat, 36
Coot, 148
Corvus corone, 74
Corvus frugilegus, 76
Corvus monedula, 72
Crested Lark, 8
Crested Tit, 52
Crossbill, 94
Crow, Carrion, 74
Crow, Hooded, 74
Cuckoo, 110
Cuculus canorus, 110
Cygnus cygnus, 136
Cygnus olor, 134
Delichon urbica, 8
Dendrocopos major, 106
Dendrocopos medius, 108
Dendrocopos minor, 108
Dipper, 16
Dove, Collared, 128
Dove, Stock, 126
Dove, Turtle, 128
Duck, Tufted, 144
Dunnock, 22
Emberiza cirlus, 98
Emberiza citrinella, 96
Emberiza hortulana, 98
Erithacus rubecula, 18
Falco subbuteo, 122
Falco tinnunculus, 120
Feral Pigeon, 126
Ficedula albicollis, 46
Ficedula hypoleuca, 46
Ficedula parva, 48
Fieldfare, 28
Firecrest, 44
Flycatcher, Collared, 46
Flycatcher, Pied, 46
Flycatcher, Red-breasted, 48
Flycatcher, Spotted, 48
Fringilla coelebs, 80
Fringilla montifringilla, 82
Fulica atra, 148
Gadwall, 142
Galerida cristata, 8
Gallinula chloropus, 148
Garden Warbler, 34
Garrulus glandarius, 68
Glaucidium passerinum, 118
Goldcrest, 44
Golden Oriole, 66
Goldeneye, 146
Goldfinch, 88
Goosander, 146

Goose, Bar-headed, 138
Goose, Canada, 136
Goose, Greylag, 138
Great Crested Grebe, 130
Great Spotted Woodpecker, 106
Great Tit, 54
Grebe, Great Crested, 130
Grebe, Little, 130
Green Woodpecker, 104
Greenfinch, 86
Grey Heron, 132
Grey Wagtail, 14
Grey-headed Woodpecker, 104
Greylag Goose, 138
Grosbeak, Pine, 94
Gull, Black-headed, 150
Gull, Common, 150
Hawfinch, 82
Heron, Grey, 132
Hippolais icterina, 32
Hirundo rustica, 10
Hobby, 122
Hooded Crow, 74
Hoopoe, 102
House Martin, 8
House Sparrow, 78
Icterine Warbler, 32
Jackdaw, 72
Jay, 68
Jay, Siberian, 70
Jynx torquilla, 102
Kestrel, 120
Kingfisher, 100
Lanius collurio, 62
Lanius senator, 62
Lark, Crested, 8
Larus canus, 150
Larus ridibundus, 150
Lesser Spotted Woodpecker, 108
Lesser Whitethroat, 36
Linnet, 92
Little Grebe, 130
Little Owl, 118
Long-eared Owl, 116
Long-tailed Tit, 56
Loxia curvirostra, 94
Lullula arborea, 6
Luscinia luscinia, 20
Luscinia megarhynchos, 20
Magpie, 72
Mallard, 140
Mandarin, 142
Marsh Tit, 50
Martin, House, 8

Mergus merganser, 146
Middle Spotted Woodpecker, 108
Mistle Thrush, 30
Moorhen, 148
Motacilla alba, 12
Motacilla cinerea, 14
Motacilla flava, 12
Mute Swan, 134
Nightingale, 20
Nightingale, Thrush, 20
Nucifraga caryocatactes, 70
Nutcracker, 70
Nuthatch, 58
Oriole, Golden, 66
Oriolus oriolus, 66
Ortolan Bunting, 98
Otus scops, 116
Owl, Barn, 112
Owl, Little, 118
Owl, Long-eared, 116
Owl, Pygmy, 118
Owl, Scops, 116
Owl, Tawny, 114
Parus ater, 56
Parus caeruleus, 52
Parus cristatus, 52
Parus major, 54
Parus montanus, 50
Parus palustris, 50
Passer domesticus, 78
Passer montanus, 76
Perisoreus infaustus, 70
Phasianus colchicus, 124
Pheasant, 124
Phoenicurus ochruros, 22
Phoenicurus phoenicurus, 24
Phylloscopus collybita, 42
Phylloscopus sibilatrix, 40
Phylloscopus trochilus, 42
Pica pica, 72
Picus canus, 104
Picus viridis, 104
Pied Flycatcher, 46
Pied Wagtail, 12
Pigeon, Feral, 126
Pine Grosbeak, 94
Pinicola enucleator, 94
Pochard, 144
Podiceps cristatus, 130
Prunella modularis, 22
Pygmy Owl, 118
Pyrrhula pyrrhula, 90
Red-backed Shrike, 62

Red-breasted Flycatcher, 48
Redpoll, 88
Redstart, 24
Redstart, Black, 22
Redwing, 28
Reed Warbler, 34
Regulus ignicapillus, 44
Regulus regulus, 44
Robin, 18
Rook, 76
Rosefinch, Common, 92
Sardinian Warbler, 40
Scops Owl, 116
Serin, 84
Serinus serinus, 84
Short-toed Treecreeper, 60
Shrike, Red-backed, 62
Shrike, Woodchat, 62
Siberian Jay, 70
Siskin, 84
Sitta europaea, 58
Skylark, 6
Song Thrush, 30
Sparrow, House, 78
Sparrow, Tree, 76
Sparrowhawk, 122
Spotless Starling, 66
Spotted Flycatcher, 48
Starling, 64
Starling, Spotless, 66
Stock Dove, 126
Stork, White, 132
Streptopelia decaocto, 128
Streptopelia turtur, 128
Strix aluco, 114
Sturnus unicolor, 66
Sturnus vulgaris, 64
Swallow, 10
Swan, Mute, 134
Swan, Whooper, 136
Swift, 100
Sylvia atricapilla, 38
Sylvia borin, 34
Sylvia communis, 36
Sylvia curruca, 36
Sylvia melanocephala, 40
Tachybaptus ruficollis, 130
Tawny Owl, 114
Thrush Nightingale, 20
Thrush, Mistle, 30
Thrush, Song, 30
Tit, Blue, 52
Tit, Coal, 56
Tit, Crested, 52
Tit, Great, 54
Tit, Long-tailed, 56

Tit, Marsh, 50
Tit, Willow, 50
Tree Sparrow, 76
Treecreeper, 60
Treecreeper, Short-toed, 60
Troglodytes troglodytes, 16
Tufted Duck, 144
Turdus iliacus, 28
Turdus merula, 26
Turdus philomelos, 30
Turdus pilaris, 28
Turdus viscivorus, 30
Turtle Dove, 128
Tyto alba, 112
Upupa epops, 102
Wagtail, Grey, 14
Wagtail, Pied, 12
Wagtail, Yellow, 12
Warbler, Garden, 34
Warbler, Icterine, 32
Warbler, Reed, 34
Warbler, Sardinian, 40
Warbler, Willow, 42
Warbler, Wood, 40
Waxwing, 14
White Stork, 132
Whitethroat, Common, 36
Whitethroat, Lesser, 36
Whooper Swan, 136
Willow Tit, 50
Willow Warbler, 42
Wood Warbler, 40
Woodchat Shrike, 62
Woodlark, 6
Woodpecker, Great Spotted, 106
Woodpecker, Green, 104
Woodpecker, Grey-headed, 104
Woodpecker, Lesser Spotted, 108
Woodpecker, Middle Spotted, 108
Woodpigeon, 124
Wren, 16
Wryneck, 102
Yellow Wagtail, 12
Yellowhammer, 96

FURTHER READING

Burton, R. (1990) *The RSPB Birdfeeder Handbook*. (Dorling Kindersley)

du Feu, C. (1993) *Nestboxes* (BTO Guide No. 23). 2nd edition. BTO

Heinzel, H., Fitter, R. & Parslow, J. (1995) Collins Pocket Guide *Birds of Britain and Europe with North Africa and the Middle East*. 5th edition. HarperCollins

Jonsson, L. (1992) *Birds of Europe with North Africa and the Middle East*. Christopher Helm

Nicolai, J., Singer, D. and Wothe, K. (1994) *Collins Nature Guide Birds of Britain and Europe*. HarperCollins

Pemberton, J. E., *The Birdwatcher's Yearbook and Diary*. Buckingham Press

FURTHER LISTENING

Couzens, D. and Wyatt, J. *Teach Yourself Bird Sounds* (8 cassettes to end of 1995 arranged by habitat; total of 12 planned). Waxwing Associates

Kettle, R. *British Bird Songs and Calls* and *More British Bird Sounds* (2 cassettes). British Library National Sound Archive

Roché, J. C. *Bird Songs Of Britain and Europe* (4 CDs or 4 cassettes); *Our Favourite Garden Birds* (1 CD or cassette). Sittelle/WildSounds

Sample, G. *Field Guide to Bird Songs and Calls of Britain and Northern Europe* (2 CDs). HarperCollins

THE PHOTOGRAPHS

Bethge: 23/1, 24 29/3, 37/2, 39/1, 3, 69/1, 77/3, 83/4, 91/2, 103/3; Danegger: 19/3, 65/1, 73/3, 78, 83/3, 105/2, 125/1, 126, 131/1, 133/2, 135/1, 149/1, 151/1, U4/u.r.: Limbrunner: U1/u.l., U2/1.r.l., 1/1.R.r.r., 7/1, 4, 15/1, 22, 31/1, 32, 35/1, 2, 36, 38, 40, 42, 54, 58, 61/1, 63/2, 68, 74, 93/4, 99/1, 106, 112, 120, 121/1, 122, 124, 137/1, 140, 147/1, 2, 148, 149/3, 151/3, U4/u.m.; Silvestris:U2/2.R.r. (Hosking), U2/2.R/l. (Wilmshurst), U2/3. R.r. (Sohns), U2/4.R.l. (Arndt), 1/2.R.l., 1/2. R.r. (Lehmann),1/3. R.l. (Walz), 1/4, R.r. (Lenz), 9/3 (Brehm), 12 (Brandt) 15/2 (Pollin), 16 (Wilmshurst), 19/2 (Wilmshurst), 23/3 (Heitmann), 27/2 (Wilmshurst), 27/3 (Sohns), 30 (Lone), 31 (Thielscher), 35/3 (Wilmshurst), 39/2 (Wilmshurst), 41/1 (Chini), 43/2 (Schulz), 47/2 (Gerlach), 47/3 (Nill), 51/1 (Thielscher), 52 (Happenhofer), 53/3 (Nill), 55/1 (Wilmshurst), 55/2 (Brandt), 55/3 (Heitmann), 57/4 (Hosking), 59/1 (Cramm), 60 (Lenz), 61/2 (Kriso), 64 (Eckert), 65/3 (Lane), 67/2 (Nill), 67/4 (Jakobi), 69/1 u.2 (Wilmshurst), 71/1 (Schiersmann), 77/2 (Schulz), 81/1 (Schmidt), 81/2 (Sohns), 81/3, 87/3 (Willner), 90 (Pforr), 91/3 (Wilmshurst 101/2 (Schmidt), 103/4 (Nill), 105/3 (Schmidt), 109/2 (Wilmshurst), 111/3 (Thielscher), 113/1 (Danegger), 113/2 (Buchhorn), 115/1 (Nill), 115/2 (Wilmshurst), 118 (Höfels), 125/2 (Wilmshurst), 127/1 (Lane), 127/2 (Lenz), 129/1 (Maier), 129/3 (Piesche 137/2 (Schiersmann), 139/2 (de Cuveland), 141/2 (Höfels), 141/3 (Thielscher), 143/3 (Wilmshurst), 145/ (Sohns), 147/3 (Arndt), 150 (Nill), U4/u.l. (Wilmshurst): Singer: U2/4.R.r 26, 29/1, 29/2, 53/1, 119/1, 130, 131/2, 131/3, 135/2; Uselmann/Bilder pur: 13 (Pott); Wendl: U1/o.r., o.l., u.m., U2/3/R.l., 2, 3, 15/3, 17/1, 19/1, 25/1, 31/3, 37/1, 45/1, 45/2, 49/4, 57/2, 3, 73/1, 77/4, 85/1, 4, 87/1, 89/1, 91/1, 93/1, 95/2, 97/3, 101/1, 103/1, 105/1, 4 111/2, 114, 117 (below), 119/2, 123 (below), 131/4, 133/1, 143/1, 145/1, 2, U4/o.l., o.r.:Wothe: 1/4.R.l., 9/4, 11/1, 13/2, 18, 25/3, 27/1, 33/1, 43/1, 51/2, 53/2, 57/1, 79/3, 95/1, 100, 103/2, 104, 108, 116, 139/3, 143/2, 151/2; Zeininge U1/u.r., U2/o.r., 1/3.R.r.r., 7/2, 3, 9/1, 2, 10, 11/2, 13/1, 3, 14, 17/2, 3, 21/1, 2, 3, 23/2, 4, 33/2, 34, 41/2, 44, 46, 47/1, 4, 48, 49/1, 2, 3, 53/4, 59/2, 62, 63, 1, 3, 4 65/2, 67/1, 3, 71/2, 75/1, 75/2, 76, 77/1 79/1, 2, 80, 82, 83/1, 2, 85/2, 3, 86, 87/ 88, 89/2, 92, 93/2, 3, 96, 97/1, 2, 99/2, 107 (below), 109/1, 110, 111/1, 121/2, 125/3, 128, 129/2, 132, 138, 139/1, 141/1, 146, 149/2

Collins Nature Guides

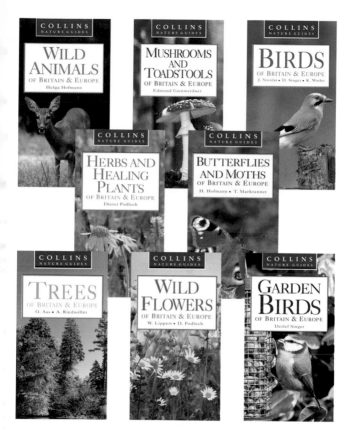

To order your copies please call our
24-hour credit card hotline 0141 772 2281

HarperCollins*Publishers*